Low Carb Slow Cooker Cookbook for Beginners

200 Wholesome Recipes to Support Blood Sugar Control, Boost Metabolism, and Promote Long-Term Health

Anna Weiland

2025

Disclaimer

This book is intended for informational and educational purposes only. The recipes and nutritional information provided in this book are not meant to replace professional medical, dietary, or nutritional advice. Please consult with a qualified healthcare provider or registered dietitian before beginning any new diet or health regimen.

The author and publisher of this book are not responsible for any adverse reactions, effects, or consequences resulting from the use of any recipes, suggestions, or procedures described herein. Individual results may vary depending on personal health, medical history, and adherence to dietary guidelines.

All ingredients and cooking methods should be handled with care. Make sure to check for food allergies or intolerances and cook food to safe internal temperatures.

Brand names or product mentions, if included, are for reference only and do not constitute endorsement or affiliation.

Table of Contents

INTRODUCTION

Welcome to the ***Low Carb Slow Cooker Cookbook for Beginners*** — your ultimate guide to delicious, nutritious, and effortless low-carb cooking!

If you're new to the low-carb lifestyle or simply looking for a more sustainable way to eat well without spending hours in the kitchen, you're in the right place. This cookbook was designed especially for busy home cooks, health-conscious individuals, and anyone who wants to enjoy flavorful meals without the carbs and the hassle.

Why Low Carb?

A low-carb diet has been shown to support weight loss, improve blood sugar levels, and boost energy by reducing the intake of processed sugars and refined carbohydrates. Instead, this way of eating focuses on wholesome, nutrient-dense foods like lean proteins, healthy fats, and non-starchy vegetables — all of which play a starring role in the recipes you'll find in this book.

Why a Slow Cooker?

Because life is busy — and cooking should be simple. The slow cooker is one of the most powerful tools in your kitchen: it transforms humble ingredients into rich, satisfying meals with minimal effort. Whether you're preparing breakfast before work, coming home to a ready-made dinner, or batch-cooking for the week, your slow cooker does the hard work for you.

All you have to do is:
- Toss in a few ingredients.
- Set the timer.
- Enjoy the magic as your home fills with irresistible aromas.

What You'll Find Inside

This cookbook is thoughtfully divided into easy-to-follow chapters covering:

- Hearty Beef, Pork, and Lamb Dishes
- Light and Flavorful Seafood Recipes
- Satisfying Poultry Favorites
- Wholesome Vegetable Mains and Sides
- Quick Appetizers and Snacks
- Comforting Soups and Stews
- Energizing Low Carb Breakfasts
- Homemade Sauces and Condiments
- Guilt-Free Low Carb Desserts
- Nourishing and Refreshing Drinks

Each recipe is designed with beginners in mind — featuring clear instructions, simple ingredients, estimated prep and cook times, and tips to help you get it just right.

A Note From the Author

I created this cookbook to make healthy eating not just achievable, but enjoyable. Whether you're cooking for yourself, your family, or entertaining friends, I want these recipes to become your go-to favorites for everyday meals and special occasions alike.

So grab your slow cooker, flip to a recipe that calls your name, and let's get cooking — the low-carb way!

Here's to flavorful meals, better health, and the joy of slow cooking.

Let's begin.

Breakfast

SLOW COOKER CHEESY EGG CASSEROLE

Servings 6 | Prep: 15 min | Cook: 240 min

This cheesy egg casserole is a delightful low-carb breakfast option, combining fluffy eggs with savory cheese and vegetables, all cooked to perfection in a slow cooker.

Equipment

Slow Cooker, Mixing Bowl, Whisk

Ingredients

- 12 large eggs
- 150 g shredded cheddar cheese
- 100 g diced bell peppers
- 100 g diced onions
- 100 g chopped spinach
- 100 ml heavy cream
- 5 g salt
- 3 g black pepper
- 10 g butter (for greasing)

Directions

1. Grease the slow cooker with butter to prevent sticking.
2. In a mixing bowl, whisk together the eggs, heavy cream, salt, and black pepper until well combined.
3. Stir in the cheddar cheese, bell peppers, onions, and spinach.
4. Pour the egg mixture into the slow cooker, spreading it evenly.
5. Cover and cook on low for 4 hours, or until the eggs are set and the top is golden.
6. Once cooked, let it cool slightly before slicing and serving.

Nutritional Information

Calories: 320, Protein: 20g, Carbohydrates: 5g, Fat: 25g, Fiber: 1g, Cholesterol: 380 mg, Salt: 450 mg, Potassium: 350 mg

KETO-FRIENDLY SAUSAGE AND SPINACH QUICHE

Servings 4 | Prep: 15 min | Cook: 180 min

This delicious keto-friendly quiche combines savory sausage with fresh spinach, all cooked to perfection in a slow cooker. It's a perfect low-carb breakfast option that is both satisfying and nutritious.

Equipment

Slow Cooker, Mixing Bowl, Whisk

Ingredients

- 200 g Sausage, crumbled
- 100 g Fresh Spinach, chopped
- 6 Large Eggs
- 100 ml Heavy Cream
- 100 g Cheddar Cheese, shredded
- 1 tsp Salt
- 1/2 tsp Black Pepper
- 1/2 tsp Garlic Powder

Directions

1. In a mixing bowl, whisk together the eggs, heavy cream, salt, black pepper, and garlic powder until well combined.
2. Add the crumbled sausage, chopped spinach, and shredded cheddar cheese to the egg mixture. Stir until all ingredients are evenly distributed.
3. Lightly grease the inside of the slow cooker with a bit of oil or cooking spray.
4. Pour the egg mixture into the slow cooker, spreading it evenly.
5. Cover and cook on low for 3 hours, or until the quiche is set and the edges are golden brown.
6. Allow to cool slightly before slicing and serving.

Nutritional Information

Calories: 350, Protein: 25g, Carbohydrates: 4g, Fat: 28g, Fiber: 1g, Cholesterol: 250 mg, Salt: 600 mg, Potassium: 350 mg

SLOW COOKER COCONUT CHIA PUDDING

Servings 4 | Prep: 10 min | Cook: 240 min

Indulge in a creamy, satisfying breakfast with this Slow Cooker Coconut Chia Pudding. It's a low-carb delight that combines the richness of coconut milk with the nutritional powerhouse of chia seeds, perfect for a healthy start to your day.

Equipment

Slow Cooker, Mixing Bowl, Whisk

Ingredients

- 400 ml Coconut Milk
- 60 g Chia Seeds
- 30 g Unsweetened Shredded Coconut
- 15 ml Vanilla Extract
- 10 g Erythritol (or preferred sweetener)
- 1 g Salt

Directions

1. In a mixing bowl, whisk together coconut milk, vanilla extract, erythritol, and salt until well combined.
2. Stir in chia seeds and shredded coconut, ensuring they are evenly distributed.
3. Pour the mixture into the slow cooker and cover.
4. Cook on low for 4 hours, stirring occasionally to prevent clumping.
5. Once thickened, transfer to serving bowls and let cool slightly before serving.
6. Optionally, garnish with fresh berries or nuts before serving.

Nutritional Information

Calories: 210, Protein: 4g, Carbohydrates: 8g, Fat: 18g, Fiber: 6g, Cholesterol: 0 mg, Salt: 150 mg, Potassium: 220 mg

LOW CARB BACON AND EGG MUFFINS

Servings 6 | Prep: 10 min | Cook: 120 min

These savory muffins combine the classic flavors of bacon and eggs into a convenient, low-carb breakfast option, perfect for busy mornings.

Equipment

Slow Cooker, Muffin Liners, Mixing Bowl

Ingredients

- 6 large eggs
- 100 g bacon, cooked and crumbled
- 50 g cheddar cheese, shredded
- 50 ml heavy cream
- 30 g spinach, chopped
- 5 g baking powder
- Salt and pepper to taste

Directions

1. In a mixing bowl, whisk together the eggs, heavy cream, baking powder, salt, and pepper until well combined.
2. Stir in the crumbled bacon, shredded cheddar cheese, and chopped spinach.
3. Line the slow cooker with muffin liners and evenly distribute the egg mixture into each liner.
4. Cover and cook on low for 2 hours, or until the muffins are set and cooked through.
5. Carefully remove the muffins from the slow cooker and let them cool slightly before serving.

Nutritional Information

Calories: 180, Protein: 12g, Carbohydrates: 2g, Fat: 14g, Fiber: 0g, Cholesterol: 180 mg, Salt: 300 mg, Potassium: 150 mg

SLOW COOKER CINNAMON ALMOND PORRIDGE

Servings 4 | Prep: 10 min | Cook: 240 min

Wake up to the comforting aroma of cinnamon and almonds with this creamy, low-carb porridge. Perfect for a cozy morning, this dish combines the nutty richness of almonds with the warmth of cinnamon, all effortlessly prepared in your slow cooker.

Equipment

Slow Cooker, Measuring Cups, Mixing Spoon

Ingredients

- 200 g Almond Flour
- 500 ml Unsweetened Almond Milk
- 50 g Chia Seeds
- 30 g Erythritol (or preferred low-carb sweetener)
- 5 g Ground Cinnamon
- 2 g Vanilla Extract
- 2 g Salt
- 30 g Sliced Almonds (for garnish)

Directions

1. In the slow cooker, combine almond flour, almond milk, chia seeds, erythritol, ground cinnamon, vanilla extract, and salt.
2. Stir the mixture well to ensure all ingredients are evenly distributed.
3. Cover and cook on low for 4 hours, stirring occasionally to prevent sticking.
4. Once cooked, give the porridge a final stir and adjust sweetness if necessary.
5. Serve warm, garnished with sliced almonds.

Nutritional Information

Calories: 250, Protein: 10g, Carbohydrates: 8g, Fat: 20g, Fiber: 6g, Cholesterol: 0 mg, Salt: 150 mg, Potassium: 250 mg

KETO SAUSAGE GRAVY WITH BISCUITS

Servings 4 | Prep: 15 min | Cook: 180 min

Indulge in a hearty breakfast with this rich and creamy keto sausage gravy served over fluffy low-carb biscuits. Perfect for a satisfying start to your day.

Equipment

Slow Cooker, Mixing Bowl, Whisk

Ingredients

- 500 g ground sausage
- 250 ml heavy cream
- 200 ml chicken broth
- 100 g almond flour
- 50 g unsalted butter
- 2 g garlic powder
- 2 g onion powder
- 2 g salt
- 2 g black pepper
- 5 g baking powder
- 2 large eggs

Directions

1. In a slow cooker, brown the ground sausage on high heat until fully cooked.
2. Add heavy cream, chicken broth, garlic powder, onion powder, salt, and black pepper to the sausage. Stir well.
3. In a mixing bowl, combine almond flour, baking powder, and a pinch of salt. Add butter and eggs, mixing until a dough forms.
4. Shape the dough into small biscuits and place them on top of the sausage mixture in the slow cooker.
5. Cover and cook on low for 3 hours, until the biscuits are cooked through and the gravy is thickened.
6. Serve hot, spooning the sausage gravy over the biscuits.

Nutritional Information

Calories: 450, Protein: 20g, Carbohydrates: 8g, Fat: 38g, Fiber: 3g, Cholesterol: 120 mg, Salt: 600 mg, Potassium: 250 mg

SLOW COOKER CHEDDAR AND BROCCOLI SCRAMBLE

Start your day with a creamy and cheesy scramble that combines the goodness of broccoli and cheddar, all effortlessly cooked in your slow cooker.

Equipment

Slow Cooker, Whisk, Mixing Bowl

Ingredients

- 200 g Broccoli florets
- 6 large Eggs
- 100 ml Heavy cream
- 150 g Cheddar cheese, shredded
- 1 g Salt
- 1 g Black pepper
- 10 g Butter

Directions

1. Grease the slow cooker with butter to prevent sticking.
2. In a mixing bowl, whisk together eggs, heavy cream, salt, and black pepper until well combined.
3. Add broccoli florets and half of the shredded cheddar cheese to the egg mixture, stirring gently.
4. Pour the mixture into the slow cooker and sprinkle the remaining cheddar cheese on top.
5. Cover and cook on low for 2 hours, or until the eggs are set and the cheese is melted.
6. Serve warm, garnished with additional cheese or herbs if desired.

Nutritional Information

Calories: 320, Protein: 18g, Carbohydrates: 5g, Fat: 26g, Fiber: 2g, Cholesterol: 250 mg, Salt: 400 mg, Potassium: 350 mg

CREAMY LOW CARB YOGURT

Indulge in this creamy, homemade low-carb yogurt, perfect for a nutritious breakfast or a delightful snack. Made effortlessly in your slow cooker, it's a healthy start to your day.

Equipment

Slow Cooker, Whisk, Cheesecloth

Ingredients

- 1 liter Whole Milk
- 100 g Greek Yogurt (as a starter culture)
- 5 g Gelatin (optional, for thicker consistency)
- 5 ml Vanilla Extract
- 20 g Erythritol (or sweetener of choice)

Directions

1. Pour the whole milk into the slow cooker and heat on low for 2-3 hours until it reaches 85°C.
2. Turn off the slow cooker and allow the milk to cool to 43°C.
3. Whisk in the Greek yogurt, gelatin, vanilla extract, and erythritol until well combined.
4. Cover the slow cooker with a lid and wrap it in a towel to maintain warmth. Let it sit for 8 hours or overnight.
5. Once set, strain the yogurt through a cheesecloth for a thicker consistency, if desired.
6. Refrigerate before serving.

Nutritional Information

Calories: 120, Protein: 6g, Carbohydrates: 5g, Fat: 8g, Fiber: 0g, Cholesterol: 25mg, Salt: 80mg, Potassium: 200mg

SLOW COOKER BLUEBERRY ALMOND CRUMBLE

This delightful slow cooker blueberry almond crumble is a perfect low-carb breakfast option, combining the sweetness of blueberries with the nutty crunch of almonds.

Equipment

Slow Cooker, Mixing Bowl, Measuring Cups

Ingredients

- 500 g fresh blueberries
- 100 g almond flour
- 50 g sliced almonds
- 50 g unsweetened shredded coconut
- 60 ml coconut oil, melted
- 30 ml sugar-free maple syrup
- 1 tsp vanilla extract
- 1/2 tsp ground cinnamon
- 1/4 tsp salt

Directions

1. Lightly grease the slow cooker with a bit of coconut oil.
2. In a mixing bowl, combine almond flour, sliced almonds, shredded coconut, melted coconut oil, sugar-free maple syrup, vanilla extract, cinnamon, and salt. Mix until crumbly.
3. Spread the blueberries evenly at the bottom of the slow cooker.
4. Sprinkle the almond mixture over the blueberries, ensuring even coverage.
5. Cover and cook on low for 3 hours, or until the topping is golden and the blueberries are bubbly.
6. Allow to cool slightly before serving.

Nutritional Information

Calories: 250, Protein: 5g, Carbohydrates: 12g, Fat: 22g, Fiber: 5g, Cholesterol: 0 mg, Salt: 150 mg, Potassium: 150 mg

BACON-WRAPPED AVOCADO EGG CUPS

These savory bacon-wrapped avocado egg cups are a delightful low-carb breakfast option, combining creamy avocado with protein-rich eggs, all enveloped in crispy bacon. Perfect for a satisfying start to your day.

Equipment

Slow Cooker, Mixing Bowl, Knife

Ingredients

- 8 slices (200g) bacon
- 2 large (400g) avocados
- 4 large (200g) eggs
- 1g salt
- 1g black pepper
- 10g fresh chives, chopped (optional)

Directions

1. Cut avocados in half and remove the pits. Scoop out a small portion of the flesh to create space for the eggs.
2. Wrap each avocado half with two slices of bacon, securing with toothpicks if necessary.
3. Place the wrapped avocados in the slow cooker.
4. Crack an egg into each avocado half, seasoning with salt and pepper.
5. Cover and cook on low for 2 hours, or until the eggs are set to your liking.
6. Garnish with chopped chives before serving, if desired.

Nutritional Information

Calories: 350, Protein: 15g, Carbohydrates: 5g, Fat: 30g, Fiber: 4g, Cholesterol: 210mg, Salt: 400mg, Potassium: 700mg

KETO-FRIENDLY FRENCH TOAST CASSEROLE

Servings 6 | Prep: 15 min | Cook: 240 min

This delightful keto-friendly French toast casserole offers a comforting breakfast experience with a low-carb twist, perfect for slow mornings or weekend brunches.

Equipment

Slow Cooker, Mixing Bowl, Whisk

Ingredients

- 300 g almond flour bread, cubed
- 200 ml unsweetened almond milk
- 4 large eggs
- 50 g cream cheese, softened
- 30 g erythritol sweetener
- 1 tsp vanilla extract
- 1 tsp ground cinnamon
- 30 g butter, melted

Directions

1. Grease the slow cooker with a small amount of butter to prevent sticking.
2. In a mixing bowl, whisk together the eggs, almond milk, cream cheese, erythritol, vanilla extract, and cinnamon until smooth.
3. Place the cubed almond flour bread into the slow cooker and pour the egg mixture over the top, ensuring all pieces are well-coated.
4. Drizzle the melted butter over the mixture.
5. Cover and cook on low for 4 hours or until the casserole is set and slightly golden on top.
6. Serve warm, optionally topped with a sprinkle of cinnamon or a dollop of whipped cream.

Nutritional Information

Calories: 280, Protein: 10g, Carbohydrates: 6g, Fat: 24g, Fiber: 3g, Cholesterol: 150 mg, Salt: 220 mg, Potassium: 120 mg

SLOW COOKER PUMPKIN SPICE PUDDING

Servings 6 | Prep: 10 min | Cook: 240 min

This creamy and aromatic pumpkin spice pudding is a delightful low-carb breakfast option, perfect for cozy mornings. The slow cooker brings out the rich flavors, making it a comforting start to your day.

Equipment

Slow Cooker, Mixing Bowl, Whisk

Ingredients

- 500 g Pumpkin Puree
- 250 ml Coconut Milk
- 3 Large Eggs
- 100 g Erythritol
- 5 g Pumpkin Spice Mix
- 5 ml Vanilla Extract
- 2 g Salt

Directions

1. In a mixing bowl, whisk together the pumpkin puree, coconut milk, and eggs until smooth.
2. Add erythritol, pumpkin spice mix, vanilla extract, and salt; mix well.
3. Pour the mixture into the slow cooker.
4. Cover and cook on low for 4 hours, or until the pudding is set and slightly firm to the touch.
5. Once cooked, allow it to cool slightly before serving.

Nutritional Information

Calories: 150, Protein: 4g, Carbohydrates: 10g, Fat: 10g, Fiber: 3g, Cholesterol: 70 mg, Salt: 150 mg, Potassium: 250 mg

CREAMY COCONUT MILK OATMEAL (LOW CARB)

Servings 4 | Prep: 10 min | Cook: 240 min

This creamy coconut milk oatmeal offers a delightful low-carb twist on a breakfast classic, perfect for a warm and satisfying start to your day.

Equipment

Slow Cooker, Measuring Cups, Mixing Spoon

Ingredients

- 400 ml Coconut Milk
- 200 g Almond Flour
- 50 g Chia Seeds
- 30 g Unsweetened Shredded Coconut
- 10 g Flaxseed Meal
- 5 ml Vanilla Extract
- 5 g Stevia or Sweetener of Choice
- 2 g Ground Cinnamon
- 1 g Salt

Directions

1. Combine coconut milk, almond flour, chia seeds, shredded coconut, and flaxseed meal in the slow cooker.
2. Stir in vanilla extract, stevia, ground cinnamon, and salt until well mixed.
3. Cover and cook on low for 4 hours, stirring occasionally to prevent sticking.
4. Once cooked, give it a final stir and adjust sweetness if necessary.
5. Serve warm, optionally garnished with additional shredded coconut or nuts.

Nutritional Information

Calories: 320, Protein: 8g, Carbohydrates: 12g, Fat: 28g, Fiber: 8g, Cholesterol: 0 mg, Salt: 150 mg, Potassium: 300 mg

KETO CHORIZO BREAKFAST SCRAMBLE

Servings 4 | Prep: 10 min | Cook: 180 min

Start your day with a flavorful and satisfying keto breakfast that combines spicy chorizo with creamy eggs, all cooked to perfection in a slow cooker.

Equipment

Slow Cooker, Mixing Bowl, Whisk

Ingredients

- 200 g Chorizo, sliced
- 8 large Eggs
- 100 ml Heavy Cream
- 100 g Cheddar Cheese, shredded
- 50 g Bell Pepper, diced
- 30 g Onion, diced
- 10 g Butter
- Salt and Pepper to taste

Directions

1. Preheat the slow cooker by setting it on low.
2. In a mixing bowl, whisk together eggs, heavy cream, salt, and pepper.
3. Melt butter in a pan over medium heat, then add chorizo, bell pepper, and onion. Sauté until the vegetables are soft.
4. Transfer the sautéed mixture to the slow cooker.
5. Pour the egg mixture over the chorizo and vegetables. Stir gently to combine.
6. Sprinkle shredded cheddar cheese on top.
7. Cover and cook on low for 3 hours, or until the eggs are set.

Nutritional Information

Calories: 450, Protein: 25g, Carbohydrates: 4g, Fat: 38g, Fiber: 1g, Cholesterol: 320 mg, Salt: 800 mg, Potassium: 350 mg

SLOW COOKER EGG AND CHEESE BAKE

Servings 6 | Prep: 10 min | Cook: 180 min

This delightful egg and cheese bake is a perfect low-carb breakfast option, offering a creamy and cheesy start to your day, all effortlessly prepared in your slow cooker.

Equipment

Slow Cooker, Mixing Bowl, Whisk

Ingredients

- 12 large eggs (approximately 600g)
- 150g cheddar cheese, shredded
- 100g spinach, chopped
- 100ml heavy cream
- 1 medium red bell pepper, diced (about 120g)
- 1 small onion, finely chopped (about 70g)
- 1 tsp salt
- 0.5 tsp black pepper

Directions

1. In a mixing bowl, whisk together the eggs, heavy cream, salt, and black pepper until well combined.
2. Stir in the cheddar cheese, spinach, red bell pepper, and onion.
3. Lightly grease the slow cooker with a bit of oil or cooking spray.
4. Pour the egg mixture into the slow cooker, spreading it evenly.
5. Cover and cook on low for 3 hours, or until the eggs are set and the edges are golden.
6. Once cooked, let it cool slightly before slicing and serving.

Nutritional Information

Calories: 280, Protein: 18g, Carbohydrates: 4g, Fat: 22g, Fiber: 1g, Cholesterol: 320mg, Salt: 450mg, Potassium: 350mg

SPICED CHAI COCONUT BREAKFAST BOWL

Servings 4 | Prep: 10 min | Cook: 240 min

This warm and comforting breakfast bowl combines the aromatic spices of chai with the creamy richness of coconut, perfect for a cozy morning start.

Equipment

Slow Cooker, Mixing Bowl, Whisk

Ingredients

- 400 ml Coconut Milk
- 200 ml Water
- 100 g Chia Seeds
- 50 g Unsweetened Shredded Coconut
- 2 g Ground Cinnamon
- 1 g Ground Cardamom
- 1 g Ground Ginger
- 1 g Ground Cloves
- 1 g Ground Nutmeg
- 5 ml Vanilla Extract
- 20 g Erythritol or Sweetener of Choice

Directions

1. In a mixing bowl, whisk together coconut milk, water, and vanilla extract until well combined.
2. Add chia seeds, shredded coconut, erythritol, cinnamon, cardamom, ginger, cloves, and nutmeg. Stir thoroughly.
3. Pour the mixture into the slow cooker.
4. Cook on low for 4 hours, stirring occasionally to prevent clumping.
5. Once thickened, serve warm or allow to cool and refrigerate for a chilled version.

Nutritional Information

Calories: 250, Protein: 5g, Carbohydrates: 10g, Fat: 22g, Fiber: 8g, Cholesterol: 0 mg, Salt: 20 mg, Potassium: 250 mg

SLOW COOKER MUSHROOM AND CHEESE OMELET

Servings 4 | Prep: 10 min | Cook: 120 min

A delightful and fluffy omelet, packed with savory mushrooms and gooey cheese, perfect for a low-carb breakfast that practically cooks itself.

Equipment

Slow Cooker, Mixing Bowl, Whisk

Ingredients

- 200 g Mushrooms, sliced
- 8 large Eggs
- 100 ml Heavy Cream
- 150 g Cheddar Cheese, shredded
- 50 g Spinach, chopped
- 1 tsp Salt
- 1/2 tsp Black Pepper
- 1 tbsp Olive Oil

Directions

1. Lightly grease the slow cooker with olive oil.
2. In a mixing bowl, whisk together eggs, heavy cream, salt, and black pepper.
3. Stir in mushrooms, spinach, and half of the cheddar cheese.
4. Pour the mixture into the slow cooker and sprinkle the remaining cheese on top.
5. Cover and cook on low for 2 hours, or until the omelet is set and the cheese is melted.
6. Serve warm, garnished with fresh herbs if desired.

Nutritional Information

Calories: 320, Protein: 20g, Carbohydrates: 5g, Fat: 25g, Fiber: 1g, Cholesterol: 280 mg, Salt: 500 mg, Potassium: 400 mg

KETO CHOCOLATE ALMOND GRANOLA

Servings 8 | Prep: 10 min | Cook: 120 min

Indulge in a crunchy, chocolatey breakfast treat that's low in carbs and high in flavor. Perfect for a quick morning meal or a satisfying snack.

Equipment

Slow Cooker, Mixing Bowl, Baking Sheet

Ingredients

- 200 g Almonds, chopped
- 100 g Walnuts, chopped
- 50 g Unsweetened Cocoa Powder
- 100 g Unsweetened Coconut Flakes
- 50 g Chia Seeds
- 100 ml Coconut Oil, melted
- 50 g Erythritol or preferred low-carb sweetener
- 1 tsp Vanilla Extract
- 1/2 tsp Salt

Directions

1. In a mixing bowl, combine almonds, walnuts, cocoa powder, coconut flakes, and chia seeds.
2. In a separate bowl, whisk together melted coconut oil, erythritol, vanilla extract, and salt.
3. Pour the wet mixture over the dry ingredients and stir until well coated.
4. Transfer the mixture to the slow cooker and spread evenly.
5. Cook on low for 2 hours, stirring every 30 minutes to ensure even cooking.
6. Once done, spread the granola on a baking sheet to cool and crisp up.
7. Store in an airtight container for up to two weeks.

Nutritional Information

Calories: 250, Protein: 6g, Carbohydrates: 8g, Fat: 22g, Fiber: 5g, Cholesterol: 0 mg, Salt: 100 mg, Potassium: 200 mg

SLOW COOKER ZUCCHINI PANCAKES

Servings 4 | Prep: 15 min | Cook: 120 min

These savory zucchini pancakes are a delightful low-carb breakfast option, perfect for a leisurely morning. The slow cooker ensures they are tender and flavorful, with a hint of cheese and herbs.

Equipment

Slow Cooker, Grater, Mixing Bowl

Ingredients

- 500 g Zucchini, grated
- 100 g Almond flour
- 100 g Parmesan cheese, grated
- 3 Eggs
- 5 g Baking powder
- 5 g Garlic powder
- 5 g Dried oregano
- Salt and pepper to taste
- 30 ml Olive oil

Directions

1. Grate the zucchini and squeeze out excess moisture using a clean kitchen towel.
2. In a mixing bowl, combine the zucchini, almond flour, Parmesan cheese, eggs, baking powder, garlic powder, oregano, salt, and pepper. Mix well until combined.
3. Grease the slow cooker with olive oil.
4. Pour the zucchini mixture into the slow cooker, spreading it evenly.
5. Cover and cook on low for 2 hours, or until the pancakes are set and lightly golden.
6. Carefully remove the pancakes from the slow cooker and let them cool slightly before serving.

Nutritional Information

Calories: 250, Protein: 15g, Carbohydrates: 8g, Fat: 18g, Fiber: 3g, Cholesterol: 120 mg, Salt: 300 mg, Potassium: 450 mg

CHEESY CAULIFLOWER BREAKFAST SKILLET

Servings 4 | Prep: 10 min | Cook: 180 min

Start your day with this creamy, cheesy cauliflower breakfast skillet, a low-carb delight that combines the richness of cheese with the subtle flavors of cauliflower, all cooked to perfection in your slow cooker.

Equipment

Slow Cooker, Mixing Bowl, Whisk

Ingredients

- 500 g cauliflower florets
- 200 g cheddar cheese, shredded
- 100 ml heavy cream
- 4 large eggs
- 50 g onion, finely chopped
- 2 cloves garlic, minced
- 5 g salt
- 2 g black pepper
- 10 g butter

Directions

1. Grease the slow cooker with butter to prevent sticking.
2. In a mixing bowl, whisk together the eggs, heavy cream, salt, and black pepper until well combined.
3. Place the cauliflower florets, onion, and garlic in the slow cooker. Pour the egg mixture over the top.
4. Sprinkle the shredded cheddar cheese evenly over the mixture.
5. Cover and cook on low for 3 hours, or until the eggs are set and the cheese is melted and bubbly.
6. Serve hot, garnished with fresh herbs if desired.

Nutritional Information

Calories: 320, Protein: 18g, Carbohydrates: 8g, Fat: 25g, Fiber: 3g, Cholesterol: 210 mg, Salt: 450 mg, Potassium: 450 mg

SOUPS AND STEWS

SLOW COOKER BROCCOLI CHEESE SOUP

Servings 6 | Prep: 15 min | Cook: 240 min

This creamy, comforting broccoli cheese soup is perfect for a low-carb diet, offering rich flavors with minimal effort.

Equipment

Slow Cooker, Cutting Board, Knife

Ingredients

- 500 g Broccoli, chopped
- 200 g Cheddar Cheese, shredded
- 1 liter Chicken Broth
- 200 ml Heavy Cream
- 100 g Onion, finely chopped
- 2 cloves Garlic, minced
- 30 g Butter
- Salt and Pepper, to taste

Directions

1. Add broccoli, onion, garlic, and butter to the slow cooker.
2. Pour in chicken broth and season with salt and pepper.
3. Cook on low for 4 hours until broccoli is tender.
4. Stir in heavy cream and cheddar cheese, mixing until cheese is melted.
5. Use an immersion blender to blend the soup to desired consistency.
6. Adjust seasoning if necessary and serve hot.

Nutritional Information

Calories: 320, Protein: 15g, Carbohydrates: 8g, Fat: 28g, Fiber: 3g, Cholesterol: 80mg, Salt: 600mg, Potassium: 450mg

KETO CHICKEN ZOODLE SOUP

Servings 4 | Prep: 15 min | Cook: 240 min

This comforting and flavorful soup combines tender chicken with zucchini noodles, offering a low-carb twist on a classic favorite. Perfect for a cozy meal that supports your keto lifestyle.

Equipment

Slow Cooker, Spiralizer, Knife, Cutting Board

Ingredients

- 500 g Chicken Breast, boneless and skinless
- 1 l Chicken Broth
- 200 g Zucchini, spiralized into noodles
- 100 g Carrots, sliced
- 100 g Celery, chopped
- 50 g Onion, diced
- 3 cloves Garlic, minced
- 10 ml Olive Oil
- 5 g Fresh Thyme
- 5 g Fresh Parsley, chopped
- Salt and Pepper to taste

Directions

1. Heat olive oil in a pan over medium heat. Add onion and garlic, sauté until fragrant.
2. Place chicken breast, sautéed onion, garlic, carrots, celery, thyme, salt, and pepper in the slow cooker.
3. Pour chicken broth over the ingredients. Cover and cook on low for 4 hours.
4. Remove chicken, shred with forks, and return to the slow cooker.
5. Add zucchini noodles and cook for an additional 10 minutes.
6. Stir in fresh parsley before serving.

Nutritional Information

Calories: 210, Protein: 30g, Carbohydrates: 8g, Fat: 7g, Fiber: 2g, Cholesterol: 70 mg, Salt: 600 mg, Potassium: 750 mg

CREAMY CAULIFLOWER SOUP

Servings 4 | Prep: 15 min | Cook: 240 min

This creamy cauliflower soup is a comforting, low-carb delight, perfect for a cozy meal. The slow cooker brings out the rich flavors, making it a satisfying choice for any occasion.

Equipment

Slow Cooker, Blender, Knife

Ingredients

- 1 kg cauliflower, chopped
- 200 g onion, diced
- 3 cloves garlic, minced
- 500 ml vegetable broth
- 200 ml heavy cream
- 30 g butter
- Salt and pepper to taste
- 5 g fresh thyme, chopped

Directions

1. Place the cauliflower, onion, garlic, and vegetable broth in the slow cooker.
2. Cook on low for 4 hours until the cauliflower is tender.
3. Blend the mixture until smooth using a blender.
4. Stir in the heavy cream and butter, then season with salt, pepper, and thyme.
5. Cook for an additional 15 minutes on low to heat through.

Nutritional Information

Calories: 210, Protein: 5g, Carbohydrates: 10g, Fat: 18g, Fiber: 4g, Cholesterol: 55 mg, Salt: 480 mg, Potassium: 450 mg

SLOW COOKER BEEF AND CABBAGE STEW

Servings 6 | Prep: 15 min | Cook: 480 min

A hearty and comforting stew that combines tender beef with the earthy flavors of cabbage, perfect for a low-carb meal.

Equipment

Slow Cooker, Cutting Board, Knife

Ingredients

- 1 kg Beef Chuck, cubed
- 500 g Green Cabbage, chopped
- 200 g Carrots, sliced
- 1 large Onion, diced
- 4 cloves Garlic, minced
- 500 ml Beef Broth
- 2 tbsp Tomato Paste
- 1 tbsp Olive Oil
- 1 tsp Dried Thyme
- 1 tsp Salt
- 0.5 tsp Black Pepper

Directions

1. Heat olive oil in a pan over medium heat and brown the beef cubes on all sides.
2. Transfer the beef to the slow cooker.
3. Add cabbage, carrots, onion, and garlic to the slow cooker.
4. In a bowl, mix beef broth, tomato paste, thyme, salt, and pepper, then pour over the ingredients in the slow cooker.
5. Cover and cook on low for 8 hours or until the beef is tender.
6. Stir well before serving.

Nutritional Information

Calories: 320, Protein: 35g, Carbohydrates: 10g, Fat: 15g, Fiber: 3g, Cholesterol: 90 mg, Salt: 600 mg, Potassium: 800 mg

LOW CARB CLAM CHOWDER

This creamy, low-carb clam chowder is a comforting bowl of goodness, perfect for a cozy meal. The slow cooker melds the flavors beautifully, making it a delightful, guilt-free indulgence.

Equipment

Slow Cooker, Knife, Cutting Board

Ingredients

- 500 g clams, cleaned
- 200 g cauliflower, chopped
- 150 g celery, diced
- 100 g onion, chopped
- 2 cloves garlic, minced
- 500 ml chicken broth
- 250 ml heavy cream
- 30 g butter
- 5 g thyme, fresh
- Salt and pepper to taste

Directions

1. Place clams, cauliflower, celery, onion, and garlic in the slow cooker.
2. Pour in the chicken broth and add butter and thyme. Stir to combine.
3. Cover and cook on low for 4 hours, until vegetables are tender.
4. Stir in heavy cream and season with salt and pepper.
5. Cook for an additional 30 minutes on low.
6. Serve hot, garnished with fresh thyme if desired.

Nutritional Information

Calories: 280, Protein: 15g, Carbohydrates: 8g, Fat: 22g, Fiber: 2g, Cholesterol: 80 mg, Salt: 600 mg, Potassium: 450 mg

KETO-FRIENDLY TACO SOUP

This hearty and flavorful taco soup is perfect for those on a keto diet. It's packed with spices and rich in protein, making it a satisfying meal for any time of the day.

Equipment

Slow Cooker, Skillet, Wooden Spoon

Ingredients

- 500 g ground beef
- 200 g diced tomatoes (canned)
- 150 g bell peppers, chopped
- 100 g onion, chopped
- 2 cloves garlic, minced
- 500 ml beef broth
- 50 g cream cheese
- 30 g taco seasoning (low-carb)
- 10 g chili powder
- 5 g cumin powder
- Salt and pepper to taste
- 100 g shredded cheddar cheese (for garnish)
- 30 g sour cream (for garnish)
- 20 g fresh cilantro, chopped (for garnish)

Directions

1. In a skillet, brown the ground beef over medium heat until fully cooked. Drain excess fat.
2. Transfer the cooked beef to the slow cooker.
3. Add diced tomatoes, bell peppers, onion, garlic, beef broth, cream cheese, taco seasoning, chili powder, cumin, salt, and pepper to the slow cooker. Stir well to combine.
4. Cover and cook on low for 4 hours, allowing the flavors to meld together.
5. Before serving, stir the soup to ensure the cream cheese is fully incorporated.
6. Serve hot, garnished with shredded cheddar cheese, a dollop of sour cream, and fresh cilantro.

Nutritional Information

Calories: 350, Protein: 25g, Carbohydrates: 8g, Fat: 25g, Fiber: 3g, Cholesterol: 80 mg, Salt: 600 mg, Potassium: 450 mg

BUTTERY GARLIC MUSHROOM SOUP

Servings 4 | Prep: 10 min | Cook: 240 min

This rich and creamy mushroom soup is infused with the aromatic flavors of garlic and butter, creating a comforting low-carb dish perfect for any occasion.

Equipment

Slow Cooker, Knife, Cutting Board

Ingredients

- 500 g Mushrooms, sliced
- 30 g Butter
- 4 cloves Garlic, minced
- 1 Onion, finely chopped
- 500 ml Vegetable Broth
- 100 ml Heavy Cream
- 5 g Fresh Thyme, chopped
- Salt and Pepper, to taste

Directions

1. Melt the butter in a pan over medium heat and sauté the garlic and onion until fragrant.
2. Add the mushrooms and cook until they start to brown.
3. Transfer the sautéed mixture to the slow cooker.
4. Pour in the vegetable broth and add the fresh thyme.
5. Cover and cook on low for 4 hours.
6. Stir in the heavy cream, season with salt and pepper, and cook for an additional 10 minutes.
7. Serve hot, garnished with extra thyme if desired.

Nutritional Information

Calories: 210, Protein: 5g, Carbohydrates: 8g, Fat: 18g, Fiber: 2g, Cholesterol: 50 mg, Salt: 400 mg, Potassium: 600 mg

SPICY SHRIMP AND SAUSAGE GUMBO

Servings 6 | Prep: 15 min | Cook: 240 min

This Spicy Shrimp and Sausage Gumbo is a hearty, flavorful dish that combines the rich taste of sausage with the delicate flavor of shrimp, all simmered to perfection in a slow cooker. Perfect for a low-carb diet, this gumbo is both satisfying and nutritious.

Equipment

Slow Cooker, Cutting Board, Knife

Ingredients

- 300 g shrimp, peeled and deveined
- 200 g smoked sausage, sliced
- 1 red bell pepper, chopped
- 1 green bell pepper, chopped
- 100 g celery, chopped
- 1 onion, chopped
- 3 cloves garlic, minced
- 400 g canned diced tomatoes
- 500 ml chicken broth
- 2 tsp Cajun seasoning
- 1 tsp paprika
- 1/2 tsp cayenne pepper
- Salt and pepper to taste
- 2 tbsp olive oil
- 2 tbsp fresh parsley, chopped

Directions

1. Heat olive oil in a pan over medium heat. Add sausage slices and cook until browned.
2. Transfer the sausage to the slow cooker. Add shrimp, bell peppers, celery, onion, garlic, and canned tomatoes.
3. Pour in chicken broth and stir in Cajun seasoning, paprika, cayenne pepper, salt, and pepper.
4. Cover and cook on low for 4 hours, or until vegetables are tender and flavors meld.
5. Stir in fresh parsley before serving.

Nutritional Information

Calories: 250, Protein: 22g, Carbohydrates: 10g, Fat: 14g, Fiber: 3g, Cholesterol: 150 mg, Salt: 800 mg, Potassium: 600 mg

SLOW COOKER EGG DROP SOUP

Servings 4 | Prep: 10 min | Cook: 120 min

A comforting and light soup, perfect for a low-carb diet, with delicate egg ribbons floating in a savory broth.

Equipment

Slow Cooker, Whisk, Ladle

Ingredients

- 1 liter chicken broth
- 5 ml soy sauce
- 2 g ground ginger
- 2 large eggs
- 2 g green onions, chopped
- 2 g white pepper
- 2 g salt

Directions

1. Pour the chicken broth, soy sauce, and ground ginger into the slow cooker. Stir to combine.
2. Set the slow cooker to low and cook for 2 hours.
3. In a bowl, whisk the eggs until smooth.
4. Slowly drizzle the eggs into the hot broth while stirring gently to create egg ribbons.
5. Season with white pepper and salt.
6. Ladle into bowls and garnish with chopped green onions before serving.

Nutritional Information

Calories: 80, Protein: 8g, Carbohydrates: 1g, Fat: 5g, Fiber: 0g, Cholesterol: 93mg, Salt: 500mg, Potassium: 150mg

THAI COCONUT CHICKEN SOUP

Servings 4 | Prep: 15 min | Cook: 240 min

This Thai Coconut Chicken Soup is a delightful blend of creamy coconut milk, tender chicken, and aromatic spices, all simmered to perfection in a slow cooker. It's a comforting, low-carb dish that brings the exotic flavors of Thailand to your kitchen.

Equipment

Slow Cooker, Cutting Board, Knife

Ingredients

- 500 g chicken breast, thinly sliced
- 400 ml coconut milk
- 500 ml chicken broth
- 100 g mushrooms, sliced
- 1 red bell pepper, sliced
- 30 g fresh ginger, sliced
- 2 cloves garlic, minced
- 2 tbsp fish sauce
- 1 tbsp lime juice
- 5 g red curry paste
- 10 g fresh cilantro, chopped
- 1 red chili, sliced (optional for heat)

Directions

1. Place the chicken, coconut milk, and chicken broth into the slow cooker.
2. Add mushrooms, red bell pepper, ginger, garlic, fish sauce, lime juice, and red curry paste. Stir to combine.
3. Cover and cook on low for 4 hours, or until the chicken is tender and cooked through.
4. Before serving, stir in fresh cilantro and sliced red chili, if using.
5. Serve hot, garnished with additional cilantro if desired.

Nutritional Information

Calories: 320, Protein: 28g, Carbohydrates: 10g, Fat: 20g, Fiber: 2g, Cholesterol: 65 mg, Salt: 800 mg, Potassium: 600 mg

KETO FRENCH ONION SOUP

Servings 4 | Prep: 15 min | Cook: 240 min

A rich and savory classic, this Keto French Onion Soup offers deep flavors with a low-carb twist, perfect for a comforting meal.

Equipment

Slow Cooker, Skillet, Ladle

Ingredients

- 500 g Yellow Onions, thinly sliced
- 30 g Butter
- 1.5 l Beef Broth
- 2 cloves Garlic, minced
- 5 g Fresh Thyme
- 10 ml Balsamic Vinegar
- 100 g Gruyère Cheese, grated
- Salt and Pepper to taste

Directions

1. In a skillet, melt butter over medium heat and add sliced onions. Cook until caramelized, about 15 minutes.
2. Transfer caramelized onions to the slow cooker.
3. Add beef broth, garlic, thyme, balsamic vinegar, salt, and pepper to the slow cooker. Stir to combine.
4. Cover and cook on low for 4 hours.
5. Before serving, ladle soup into bowls and top with grated Gruyère cheese.

Nutritional Information

Calories: 250, Protein: 12g, Carbohydrates: 10g, Fat: 18g, Fiber: 2g, Cholesterol: 45mg, Salt: 800mg, Potassium: 400mg

CREAMY TOMATO BASIL SOUP

Servings 4 | Prep: 10 min | Cook: 240 min

This creamy tomato basil soup is a comforting, low-carb delight that combines the rich flavors of tomatoes with the aromatic essence of fresh basil, all simmered to perfection in a slow cooker.

Equipment

Slow Cooker, Blender, Knife

Ingredients

- 800 g canned whole tomatoes
- 200 ml vegetable broth
- 100 ml heavy cream
- 30 g fresh basil leaves
- 1 medium onion, chopped (about 150 g)
- 3 cloves garlic, minced
- 15 ml olive oil
- Salt and pepper to taste

Directions

1. Heat olive oil in a pan over medium heat and sauté the onion and garlic until translucent.
2. Transfer the sautéed onion and garlic to the slow cooker.
3. Add canned tomatoes, vegetable broth, and basil leaves to the slow cooker.
4. Cover and cook on low for 4 hours.
5. Use a blender to puree the soup until smooth.
6. Stir in the heavy cream and season with salt and pepper.
7. Serve hot, garnished with additional basil if desired.

Nutritional Information

Calories: 180, Protein: 4g, Carbohydrates: 12g, Fat: 14g, Fiber: 3g, Cholesterol: 35 mg, Salt: 400 mg, Potassium: 600 mg

SLOW COOKER TURKEY AND SPINACH SOUP

Servings 6 | Prep: 15 min | Cook: 240 min

A hearty and nutritious soup that combines lean turkey with vibrant spinach, perfect for a comforting low-carb meal.

Equipment

Slow Cooker, Cutting Board, Knife

Ingredients

- 500 g ground turkey
- 200 g fresh spinach
- 1 medium onion, chopped
- 2 cloves garlic, minced
- 1 liter chicken broth
- 200 g diced tomatoes
- 1 tsp dried oregano
- 1 tsp dried basil
- Salt and pepper to taste

Directions

1. In a slow cooker, combine ground turkey, chopped onion, and minced garlic.
2. Add chicken broth, diced tomatoes, oregano, and basil. Stir well.
3. Season with salt and pepper to taste.
4. Cover and cook on low for 4 hours.
5. Add fresh spinach during the last 15 minutes of cooking. Stir until wilted.
6. Serve hot and enjoy your nutritious low-carb soup.

Nutritional Information

Calories: 180, Protein: 22g, Carbohydrates: 6g, Fat: 8g, Fiber: 2g, Cholesterol: 55 mg, Salt: 600 mg, Potassium: 650 mg

KETO CHEESEBURGER SOUP

Servings 6 | Prep: 15 min | Cook: 240 min

This rich and creamy Keto Cheeseburger Soup brings all the flavors of a classic cheeseburger into a comforting bowl, perfect for a low-carb diet.

Equipment

Slow Cooker, Skillet, Ladle

Ingredients

- 500 g Ground Beef
- 200 g Cheddar Cheese, shredded
- 150 g Cream Cheese
- 1 L Beef Broth
- 100 g Onion, chopped
- 100 g Celery, chopped
- 100 g Cauliflower, chopped
- 50 ml Heavy Cream
- 30 ml Olive Oil
- 5 g Garlic, minced
- Salt and Pepper to taste

Directions

1. Heat olive oil in a skillet over medium heat. Add ground beef and cook until browned. Drain excess fat.
2. Transfer the cooked beef to the slow cooker. Add onion, celery, cauliflower, and garlic.
3. Pour in the beef broth and stir in the cream cheese. Season with salt and pepper.
4. Cover and cook on low for 4 hours.
5. Stir in the heavy cream and shredded cheddar cheese. Cook for an additional 10 minutes until the cheese is melted.
6. Serve hot, garnished with extra cheese if desired.

Nutritional Information

Calories: 450, Protein: 30g, Carbohydrates: 6g, Fat: 35g, Fiber: 2g, Cholesterol: 110 mg, Salt: 800 mg, Potassium: 600 mg

HEARTY LOW CARB BEEF STEW

Servings 6 | Prep: 15 min | Cook: 480 min

This rich and savory beef stew is perfect for a comforting meal, packed with tender beef and low-carb vegetables, all simmered to perfection in a slow cooker.

Equipment

Slow Cooker, Cutting Board, Knife

Ingredients

- 1 kg Beef Chuck, cut into cubes
- 200 g Carrots, sliced
- 150 g Celery, chopped
- 1 large Onion, chopped
- 3 cloves Garlic, minced
- 400 ml Beef Broth
- 200 g Mushrooms, sliced
- 2 tbsp Tomato Paste
- 1 tbsp Olive Oil
- 1 tsp Dried Thyme
- 1 tsp Dried Rosemary
- Salt and Pepper to taste

Directions

1. Heat olive oil in a pan over medium heat. Brown the beef cubes on all sides.
2. Transfer the beef to the slow cooker. Add carrots, celery, onion, garlic, and mushrooms.
3. Stir in the tomato paste, beef broth, thyme, rosemary, salt, and pepper.
4. Cover and cook on low for 8 hours or until the beef is tender.
5. Adjust seasoning before serving.

Nutritional Information

Calories: 350, Protein: 35g, Carbohydrates: 10g, Fat: 20g, Fiber: 3g, Cholesterol: 90 mg, Salt: 600 mg, Potassium: 800 mg

SLOW COOKER HAM AND CABBAGE SOUP

Servings 6 | Prep: 15 min | Cook: 240 min

This hearty and comforting soup combines tender ham with fresh cabbage, creating a flavorful low-carb meal perfect for any day.

Equipment

Slow Cooker, Cutting Board, Knife

Ingredients

- 500 g ham, diced
- 1 kg cabbage, chopped
- 200 g carrots, sliced
- 1 onion, chopped
- 3 cloves garlic, minced
- 1.5 liters chicken broth
- 5 g dried thyme
- 5 g black pepper
- 2 g salt

Directions

1. Place the diced ham, chopped cabbage, sliced carrots, chopped onion, and minced garlic into the slow cooker.
2. Pour the chicken broth over the ingredients in the slow cooker.
3. Add dried thyme, black pepper, and salt. Stir to combine.
4. Cover and cook on low for 4 hours, or until the vegetables are tender.
5. Taste and adjust seasoning if necessary before serving.

Nutritional Information

Calories: 180, Protein: 18g, Carbohydrates: 10g, Fat: 7g, Fiber: 4g, Cholesterol: 40 mg, Salt: 800 mg, Potassium: 600 mg

ITALIAN SAUSAGE AND KALE SOUP

Servings 6 | Prep: 15 min | Cook: 240 min

This hearty Italian Sausage and Kale Soup is a comforting, low-carb delight, perfect for a cozy meal. The slow cooker melds the flavors beautifully, creating a rich and satisfying dish.

Equipment

Slow Cooker, Knife, Cutting Board

Ingredients

- 500 g Italian sausage, casings removed
- 200 g kale, chopped
- 1 medium onion, diced
- 3 cloves garlic, minced
- 1.5 liters chicken broth
- 200 g tomatoes, diced
- 1 tsp dried oregano
- 1 tsp dried basil
- Salt and pepper to taste

Directions

1. Brown the Italian sausage in a pan over medium heat, breaking it into small pieces.
2. Transfer the browned sausage to the slow cooker.
3. Add the chopped kale, diced onion, minced garlic, chicken broth, diced tomatoes, oregano, and basil to the slow cooker.
4. Stir the ingredients to combine, then season with salt and pepper to taste.
5. Cover and cook on low for 4 hours, or until the kale is tender and the flavors are well combined.
6. Taste and adjust seasoning if necessary before serving.

Nutritional Information

Calories: 320, Protein: 20g, Carbohydrates: 8g, Fat: 24g, Fiber: 2g, Cholesterol: 60 mg, Salt: 800 mg, Potassium: 600 mg

SPICY ROASTED RED PEPPER SOUP

Servings 4 | Prep: 15 min | Cook: 240 min

This vibrant and spicy roasted red pepper soup is a delightful blend of flavors, perfect for a cozy meal. The slow cooker enhances the depth of the roasted peppers, creating a rich and satisfying low-carb dish.

Equipment

Slow Cooker, Blender, Knife

Ingredients

- 600 g roasted red peppers, drained
- 200 g tomatoes, chopped
- 1 medium onion, chopped
- 3 cloves garlic, minced
- 500 ml vegetable broth
- 100 ml heavy cream
- 1 tsp smoked paprika
- 1/2 tsp cayenne pepper
- Salt and pepper to taste
- 15 ml olive oil

Directions

1. Heat olive oil in a pan over medium heat. Add onion and garlic, sauté until translucent.
2. Transfer onion and garlic to the slow cooker. Add roasted red peppers, tomatoes, vegetable broth, smoked paprika, cayenne pepper, salt, and pepper.
3. Cover and cook on low for 4 hours.
4. Once cooked, blend the mixture until smooth using a blender.
5. Stir in heavy cream and adjust seasoning if necessary. Serve hot.

Nutritional Information

Calories: 180, Protein: 4g, Carbohydrates: 12g, Fat: 14g, Fiber: 3g, Cholesterol: 25 mg, Salt: 600 mg, Potassium: 500 mg

KETO CHICKEN ENCHILADA SOUP

Servings 6 | Prep: 15 min | Cook: 240 min

This rich and flavorful Keto Chicken Enchilada Soup is perfect for a cozy meal, offering all the deliciousness of enchiladas without the carbs.

Equipment

Slow Cooker, Cutting Board, Knife

Ingredients

- 500 g Chicken Breast, boneless and skinless
- 400 g Canned Tomatoes, diced
- 200 g Bell Peppers, chopped
- 100 g Onion, chopped
- 2 cloves Garlic, minced
- 500 ml Chicken Broth
- 100 g Cream Cheese
- 50 g Cheddar Cheese, shredded
- 10 g Chili Powder
- 5 g Cumin
- 5 g Paprika
- Salt and Pepper, to taste

Directions

1. Place the chicken breasts at the bottom of the slow cooker.
2. Add the diced tomatoes, bell peppers, onion, and garlic over the chicken.
3. Pour in the chicken broth and add the chili powder, cumin, paprika, salt, and pepper. Stir to combine.
4. Cover and cook on low for 4 hours, or until the chicken is fully cooked and tender.
5. Remove the chicken, shred it using two forks, and return it to the slow cooker.
6. Stir in the cream cheese and cheddar cheese until melted and well combined.
7. Adjust seasoning if necessary and serve hot.

Nutritional Information

Calories: 320, Protein: 30g, Carbohydrates: 8g, Fat: 20g, Fiber: 2g, Cholesterol: 85 mg, Salt: 600 mg, Potassium: 750 mg

CREAMY ASPARAGUS SOUP

Servings 4 | Prep: 10 min | Cook: 240 min

This creamy asparagus soup is a delightful blend of fresh asparagus and aromatic herbs, perfect for a comforting low-carb meal.

Equipment

Slow Cooker, Blender, Knife

Ingredients

- 500 g asparagus, trimmed and chopped
- 1 medium onion, chopped
- 2 cloves garlic, minced
- 500 ml vegetable broth
- 200 ml heavy cream
- 15 g butter
- Salt and pepper to taste
- 5 g fresh parsley, chopped (for garnish)

Directions

1. Place asparagus, onion, garlic, and vegetable broth in the slow cooker.
2. Cook on low for 4 hours until asparagus is tender.
3. Use a blender to puree the soup until smooth.
4. Stir in heavy cream and butter, then season with salt and pepper.
5. Cook for an additional 10 minutes on low.
6. Serve hot, garnished with fresh parsley.

Nutritional Information

Calories: 220, Protein: 4g, Carbohydrates: 8g, Fat: 20g, Fiber: 3g, Cholesterol: 60 mg, Salt: 500 mg, Potassium: 400 mg

VEGETABLE MAINS AND SIDES RECIPES

SLOW COOKER CREAMED SPINACH

Servings 4 | Prep: 10 min | Cook: 120 min

This rich and creamy spinach dish is a perfect low-carb side that pairs well with any main course. The slow cooker melds the flavors beautifully, creating a comforting and nutritious dish.

Equipment

Slow Cooker, Mixing Bowl, Whisk

Ingredients

- 500 g Fresh Spinach
- 200 ml Heavy Cream
- 100 g Cream Cheese, softened
- 50 g Grated Parmesan Cheese
- 2 cloves Garlic, minced
- 30 g Butter
- Salt and Pepper to taste
- 1/2 tsp Nutmeg (optional)

Directions

1. Rinse the spinach thoroughly and place it in the slow cooker.
2. In a mixing bowl, whisk together the heavy cream, cream cheese, Parmesan cheese, minced garlic, butter, salt, pepper, and nutmeg until smooth.
3. Pour the cream mixture over the spinach in the slow cooker.
4. Cover and cook on low for 2 hours, stirring halfway through to ensure even cooking.
5. Once the spinach is tender and the sauce is creamy, adjust seasoning if necessary and serve warm.

Nutritional Information

Calories: 250, Protein: 6g, Carbohydrates: 5g, Fat: 23g, Fiber: 3g, Cholesterol: 70 mg, Salt: 300 mg, Potassium: 450 mg

GARLIC BUTTER ROASTED CAULIFLOWER

Servings 4 | Prep: 10 min | Cook: 180 min

This dish transforms simple cauliflower into a rich, buttery delight with a hint of garlic, perfect as a main or a side.

Equipment

Slow Cooker, Mixing Bowl, Spoon

Ingredients

- 1 kg Cauliflower, cut into florets
- 100 g Unsalted Butter, melted
- 5 cloves Garlic, minced
- 10 g Fresh Parsley, chopped
- 5 g Salt
- 2 g Black Pepper

Directions

1. In a mixing bowl, combine melted butter, minced garlic, salt, and black pepper.
2. Add cauliflower florets to the bowl and toss until well coated with the butter mixture.
3. Transfer the coated cauliflower to the slow cooker.
4. Cover and cook on low for 3 hours or until the cauliflower is tender.
5. Before serving, sprinkle with fresh parsley for garnish.

Nutritional Information

Calories: 180, Protein: 4g, Carbohydrates: 10g, Fat: 15g, Fiber: 4g, Cholesterol: 38 mg, Salt: 500 mg, Potassium: 450 mg

PARMESAN BRUSSEL SPROUTS

Servings 4 | Prep: 10 min | Cook: 180 min

Savor the delightful combination of tender Brussels sprouts and savory Parmesan cheese in this low-carb, slow-cooked dish. Perfect as a main or a side, it's a flavorful way to enjoy your greens.

Equipment

Slow Cooker, Mixing Bowl, Grater

Ingredients

- 500 g Brussels sprouts, halved
- 60 ml olive oil
- 100 g Parmesan cheese, grated
- 3 cloves garlic, minced
- 5 g salt
- 2 g black pepper
- 10 g fresh parsley, chopped (optional)

Directions

1. In a mixing bowl, combine Brussels sprouts, olive oil, garlic, salt, and pepper. Toss until the sprouts are well coated.
2. Transfer the mixture to the slow cooker, spreading it evenly.
3. Cook on low for 3 hours, stirring halfway through to ensure even cooking.
4. In the last 30 minutes, sprinkle the grated Parmesan cheese over the Brussels sprouts.
5. Once cooked, garnish with fresh parsley before serving, if desired.

Nutritional Information

Calories: 210, Protein: 9g, Carbohydrates: 10g, Fat: 16g, Fiber: 4g, Cholesterol: 15 mg, Salt: 400 mg, Potassium: 450 mg

CHEESY BROCCOLI CASSEROLE

Servings 4 | Prep: 10 min | Cook: 180 min

This creamy, cheesy broccoli casserole is a comforting low-carb dish perfect for any meal. The slow cooker ensures the broccoli is tender and the cheese is perfectly melted.

Equipment

Slow Cooker, Mixing Bowl, Measuring Cups and Spoons

Ingredients

- 500 g Broccoli florets
- 200 g Cheddar cheese, shredded
- 100 ml Heavy cream
- 50 g Cream cheese
- 1 clove Garlic, minced
- 5 g Salt
- 2 g Black pepper
- 10 g Butter, for greasing

Directions

1. Grease the slow cooker with butter to prevent sticking.
2. In a mixing bowl, combine heavy cream, cream cheese, garlic, salt, and pepper until smooth.
3. Place broccoli florets in the slow cooker and pour the cream mixture over them.
4. Sprinkle shredded cheddar cheese evenly on top.
5. Cover and cook on low for 3 hours, or until broccoli is tender and cheese is bubbly.
6. Stir gently before serving to mix the melted cheese throughout.

Nutritional Information

Calories: 320, Protein: 15g, Carbohydrates: 8g, Fat: 28g, Fiber: 3g, Cholesterol: 75 mg, Salt: 450 mg, Potassium: 400 mg

SLOW COOKER STUFFED BELL PEPPERS

Servings 4 | Prep: 15 min | Cook: 240 min

These slow cooker stuffed bell peppers are a delightful low-carb meal, filled with a savory mixture of ground meat and vegetables, perfect for a hearty yet healthy dinner.

Equipment

Slow Cooker, Mixing Bowl, Knife

Ingredients

- 4 large bell peppers (any color)
- 500 g ground beef or turkey
- 100 g cauliflower rice
- 100 g diced tomatoes
- 50 g chopped onion
- 2 cloves garlic, minced
- 5 g dried oregano
- 5 g dried basil
- 5 g salt
- 2 g black pepper
- 50 g shredded mozzarella cheese

Directions

1. Cut the tops off the bell peppers and remove the seeds and membranes.
2. In a mixing bowl, combine the ground meat, cauliflower rice, diced tomatoes, onion, garlic, oregano, basil, salt, and black pepper.
3. Stuff each bell pepper with the meat mixture and place them upright in the slow cooker.
4. Cover and cook on low for 4 hours, or until the peppers are tender.
5. In the last 15 minutes of cooking, sprinkle mozzarella cheese on top of each pepper and cover to melt.

Nutritional Information

Calories: 320, Protein: 28g, Carbohydrates: 12g, Fat: 18g, Fiber: 4g, Cholesterol: 70 mg, Salt: 600 mg, Potassium: 750 mg

BUTTERED ASPARAGUS SPEARS

Servings 4 | Prep: 10 min | Cook: 120 min

Tender asparagus spears bathed in rich, melted butter, offering a delightful low-carb side dish that complements any main course.

Equipment

Slow Cooker, Knife, Cutting Board

Ingredients

- 500 g Asparagus Spears
- 50 g Unsalted Butter
- 5 g Garlic, minced
- 5 ml Lemon Juice
- 2 g Salt
- 1 g Black Pepper

Directions

1. Trim the woody ends off the asparagus spears.
2. Place the asparagus in the slow cooker.
3. Melt the butter in a small saucepan over low heat, then stir in the minced garlic.
4. Pour the melted butter and garlic mixture over the asparagus.
5. Add lemon juice, salt, and black pepper. Toss to coat evenly.
6. Cover and cook on low for 2 hours or until the asparagus is tender.
7. Serve warm, garnished with additional lemon zest if desired.

Nutritional Information

Calories: 110, Protein: 2g, Carbohydrates: 4g, Fat: 10g, Fiber: 2g, Cholesterol: 20 mg, Salt: 200 mg, Potassium: 250 mg

CAULIFLOWER MAC AND CHEESE

This creamy and cheesy cauliflower dish is a low-carb twist on the classic mac and cheese, perfect for satisfying comfort food cravings without the carbs.

Equipment

Slow Cooker, Mixing Bowl, Whisk

Ingredients

- 500 g Cauliflower, cut into florets
- 200 ml Heavy Cream
- 150 g Cheddar Cheese, shredded
- 50 g Parmesan Cheese, grated
- 50 g Cream Cheese
- 1 tsp Garlic Powder
- 1 tsp Mustard Powder
- Salt and Pepper, to taste

Directions

1. Place cauliflower florets in the slow cooker.
2. In a mixing bowl, whisk together heavy cream, cheddar cheese, parmesan cheese, cream cheese, garlic powder, mustard powder, salt, and pepper until smooth.
3. Pour the cheese mixture over the cauliflower in the slow cooker.
4. Cover and cook on low for 3 hours, or until the cauliflower is tender and the cheese sauce is bubbly.
5. Stir well before serving to ensure the cauliflower is evenly coated with the cheese sauce.

Nutritional Information

Calories: 320, Protein: 15g, Carbohydrates: 8g, Fat: 28g, Fiber: 3g, Cholesterol: 85 mg, Salt: 450 mg, Potassium: 450 mg

LOW CARB RATATOUILLE

A delightful medley of Mediterranean vegetables, this low carb ratatouille is a vibrant and flavorful dish that simmers to perfection in the slow cooker, offering a healthy and satisfying meal.

Equipment

Slow Cooker, Cutting Board, Knife

Ingredients

- 200 g Eggplant, diced
- 150 g Zucchini, sliced
- 150 g Bell Pepper, chopped
- 100 g Onion, chopped
- 3 cloves Garlic, minced
- 400 g Canned Tomatoes, crushed
- 30 ml Olive Oil
- 5 g Fresh Basil, chopped
- 5 g Fresh Thyme, chopped
- Salt and Pepper to taste

Directions

1. Place the eggplant, zucchini, bell pepper, onion, and garlic in the slow cooker.
2. Pour the crushed tomatoes over the vegetables and drizzle with olive oil.
3. Add the fresh basil, thyme, salt, and pepper, stirring to combine.
4. Cover and cook on low for 4 hours, or until vegetables are tender.
5. Stir before serving and adjust seasoning if necessary.

Nutritional Information

Calories: 120, Protein: 3g, Carbohydrates: 15g, Fat: 7g, Fiber: 5g, Cholesterol: 0 mg, Salt: 300 mg, Potassium: 550 mg

SLOW COOKER ZUCCHINI LASAGNA

Servings 4 | Prep: 20 min | Cook: 240 min

A delightful low-carb twist on a classic favorite, this zucchini lasagna is layered with rich flavors and cooked to perfection in a slow cooker.

Equipment

Slow Cooker, Mandoline Slicer, Mixing Bowl

Ingredients

- 500 g zucchini, thinly sliced
- 250 g ricotta cheese
- 200 g mozzarella cheese, shredded
- 100 g parmesan cheese, grated
- 300 g ground beef
- 400 g tomato sauce
- 1 onion, finely chopped
- 2 cloves garlic, minced
- 1 tsp dried oregano
- 1 tsp dried basil
- Salt and pepper to taste

Directions

1. Brown the ground beef in a pan over medium heat, adding onion and garlic until fragrant.
2. Stir in tomato sauce, oregano, basil, salt, and pepper. Simmer for 5 minutes.
3. In the slow cooker, layer zucchini slices, ricotta cheese, beef mixture, and mozzarella cheese. Repeat layers, ending with mozzarella and parmesan on top.
4. Cover and cook on low for 4 hours or until zucchini is tender.
5. Let it rest for 10 minutes before serving.

Nutritional Information

Calories: 350, Protein: 28g, Carbohydrates: 12g, Fat: 20g, Fiber: 3g, Cholesterol: 70 mg, Salt: 600 mg, Potassium: 900 mg

SPICY EGGPLANT STEW

Servings 4 | Prep: 15 min | Cook: 240 min

This Spicy Eggplant Stew is a hearty and flavorful dish, perfect for those seeking a low-carb meal with a kick. The slow cooker melds the spices beautifully, creating a rich and satisfying stew.

Equipment

Slow Cooker, Cutting Board, Knife

Ingredients

- 500 g Eggplant, diced
- 200 g Bell Peppers, chopped
- 150 g Onion, chopped
- 3 cloves Garlic, minced
- 400 g Canned Tomatoes, diced
- 100 ml Vegetable Broth
- 15 ml Olive Oil
- 5 g Ground Cumin
- 5 g Paprika
- 2 g Red Pepper Flakes
- Salt and Pepper to taste
- Fresh Parsley, for garnish

Directions

1. Heat olive oil in a pan over medium heat. Sauté onions and garlic until fragrant.
2. Add eggplant, bell peppers, cumin, paprika, and red pepper flakes. Stir well.
3. Transfer the mixture to the slow cooker. Add canned tomatoes and vegetable broth.
4. Season with salt and pepper. Stir to combine.
5. Cover and cook on low for 4 hours, until the eggplant is tender.
6. Garnish with fresh parsley before serving.

Nutritional Information

Calories: 150, Protein: 3g, Carbohydrates: 20g, Fat: 7g, Fiber: 8g, Cholesterol: 0 mg, Salt: 300 mg, Potassium: 600 mg

CHEESY MUSHROOM CASSEROLE

Servings 4 | Prep: 15 min | Cook: 240 min

This creamy and cheesy mushroom casserole is a delightful low-carb dish that combines the earthy flavors of mushrooms with the richness of cheese, all cooked to perfection in a slow cooker.

Equipment

Slow Cooker, Mixing Bowl, Spoon

Ingredients

- 500 g mushrooms, sliced
- 200 g cream cheese, softened
- 150 g cheddar cheese, shredded
- 100 ml heavy cream
- 1 medium onion, finely chopped
- 2 cloves garlic, minced
- 1 tsp dried thyme
- Salt and pepper to taste

Directions

1. In a mixing bowl, combine the cream cheese, heavy cream, garlic, thyme, salt, and pepper until smooth.
2. Place the sliced mushrooms and chopped onion in the slow cooker.
3. Pour the cream cheese mixture over the mushrooms and onions, stirring to coat evenly.
4. Sprinkle the shredded cheddar cheese on top.
5. Cover and cook on low for 4 hours, or until the mushrooms are tender and the cheese is bubbly.
6. Serve hot as a main or side dish.

Nutritional Information

Calories: 320, Protein: 12g, Carbohydrates: 8g, Fat: 28g, Fiber: 2g, Cholesterol: 70 mg, Salt: 450 mg, Potassium: 550 mg

SLOW COOKER GREEN BEAN ALMONDINE

Servings 4 | Prep: 10 min | Cook: 180 min

A delightful low-carb side dish featuring tender green beans and crunchy almonds, perfect for any meal.

Equipment

Slow Cooker, Mixing Bowl, Measuring Cups

Ingredients

- 500 g fresh green beans, trimmed
- 60 ml olive oil
- 50 g sliced almonds
- 3 cloves garlic, minced
- 1 lemon, juiced
- Salt and pepper to taste

Directions

1. Place the green beans in the slow cooker.
2. In a mixing bowl, combine olive oil, minced garlic, lemon juice, salt, and pepper. Pour over the green beans.
3. Cover and cook on low for 3 hours, or until the beans are tender.
4. In the last 30 minutes, add the sliced almonds to the slow cooker.
5. Stir well before serving to ensure the almonds are evenly distributed.

Nutritional Information

Calories: 180, Protein: 4g, Carbohydrates: 9g, Fat: 15g, Fiber: 4g, Cholesterol: 0 mg, Salt: 150 mg, Potassium: 250 mg

BUTTERY GARLIC ROASTED RADISHES

Servings 4 | Prep: 10 min | Cook: 180 min

A delightful low-carb alternative to potatoes, these buttery garlic roasted radishes are tender, flavorful, and perfect as a side dish or a main vegetarian delight.

Equipment

Slow Cooker, Mixing Bowl, Knife

Ingredients

- 500 g radishes, trimmed and halved
- 50 g unsalted butter, melted
- 5 cloves garlic, minced
- 5 g fresh parsley, chopped
- 5 g salt
- 2 g black pepper

Directions

1. In a mixing bowl, combine the melted butter, minced garlic, salt, and black pepper.
2. Add the halved radishes to the bowl and toss until they are well coated with the butter mixture.
3. Transfer the coated radishes to the slow cooker.
4. Cover and cook on low for 3 hours, or until the radishes are tender.
5. Before serving, sprinkle with fresh parsley for garnish.

Nutritional Information

Calories: 85, Protein: 1g, Carbohydrates: 4g, Fat: 8g, Fiber: 2g, Cholesterol: 20 mg, Salt: 300 mg, Potassium: 230 mg

SPINACH & FETA STUFFED PEPPERS

Servings 4 | Prep: 15 min | Cook: 240 min

These vibrant stuffed peppers are filled with a savory mixture of spinach and feta, offering a delightful low-carb option that's both nutritious and satisfying.

Equipment

Slow Cooker, Mixing Bowl, Knife

Ingredients

- 4 large bell peppers
- 200 g fresh spinach, chopped
- 150 g feta cheese, crumbled
- 1 small onion, finely chopped
- 2 cloves garlic, minced
- 1 tbsp olive oil
- 1 tsp dried oregano
- Salt and pepper to taste

Directions

1. Cut the tops off the bell peppers and remove the seeds and membranes.
2. In a mixing bowl, combine spinach, feta, onion, garlic, olive oil, oregano, salt, and pepper. Mix well.
3. Stuff each bell pepper with the spinach and feta mixture.
4. Place the stuffed peppers upright in the slow cooker.
5. Cover and cook on low for 4 hours, or until the peppers are tender.

Nutritional Information

Calories: 180, Protein: 8g, Carbohydrates: 10g, Fat: 12g, Fiber: 3g, Cholesterol: 25mg, Salt: 400mg, Potassium: 450mg

CARAMELIZED BRUSSELS SPROUTS

Servings 4 | Prep: 10 min | Cook: 180 min

These caramelized Brussels sprouts are a delightful low-carb side dish, offering a perfect balance of sweetness and savory flavors, all achieved effortlessly in a slow cooker.

Equipment

Slow Cooker, Mixing Bowl, Wooden Spoon

Ingredients

- 500 g Brussels sprouts, halved
- 30 ml olive oil
- 20 g unsalted butter
- 30 ml balsamic vinegar
- 10 g garlic, minced
- 5 g salt
- 2 g black pepper
- 5 g fresh thyme leaves

Directions

1. In a mixing bowl, combine olive oil, balsamic vinegar, minced garlic, salt, and black pepper.
2. Add the halved Brussels sprouts to the bowl and toss until they are evenly coated with the mixture.
3. Transfer the coated Brussels sprouts to the slow cooker and dot with unsalted butter.
4. Cover and cook on low for 3 hours, stirring halfway through to ensure even caramelization.
5. Once cooked, sprinkle fresh thyme leaves over the Brussels sprouts and give a final stir before serving.

Nutritional Information

Calories: 150, Protein: 4g, Carbohydrates: 12g, Fat: 10g, Fiber: 5g, Cholesterol: 8 mg, Salt: 300 mg, Potassium: 450 mg

KETO-FRIENDLY CABBAGE SOUP

Servings 6 | Prep: 15 min | Cook: 240 min

This hearty and nourishing cabbage soup is perfect for those following a low-carb diet. Packed with flavor and nutrients, it's a comforting dish that warms you from the inside out.

Equipment

Slow Cooker, Cutting Board, Knife

Ingredients

- 1 kg Green Cabbage, chopped
- 500 g Ground Beef
- 200 g Carrots, sliced
- 150 g Celery, chopped
- 1 Onion, chopped
- 4 cloves Garlic, minced
- 1.5 l Beef Broth
- 30 ml Olive Oil
- 5 g Salt
- 3 g Black Pepper
- 5 g Dried Thyme
- 5 g Paprika

Directions

1. Heat olive oil in a pan over medium heat and brown the ground beef.
2. Transfer the beef to the slow cooker. Add cabbage, carrots, celery, onion, and garlic.
3. Pour in the beef broth and stir in salt, pepper, thyme, and paprika.
4. Cover and cook on low for 4 hours or until vegetables are tender.
5. Adjust seasoning to taste before serving.

Nutritional Information

Calories: 250, Protein: 20g, Carbohydrates: 12g, Fat: 15g, Fiber: 4g, Cholesterol: 50 mg, Salt: 600 mg, Potassium: 700 mg

LOADED CAULIFLOWER MASH

Indulge in this creamy, cheesy cauliflower mash that delivers all the comfort of traditional mashed potatoes without the carbs. Perfect as a side dish or a main course for a low-carb lifestyle.

Equipment

Slow Cooker, Blender or Food Processor, Mixing Bowl

Ingredients

- 1 kg cauliflower, chopped
- 200 ml chicken broth
- 100 g cream cheese
- 100 g shredded cheddar cheese
- 50 g unsalted butter
- 2 cloves garlic, minced
- 50 g bacon bits
- 2 tbsp fresh chives, chopped
- Salt and pepper to taste

Directions

1. Place the chopped cauliflower and minced garlic in the slow cooker. Pour the chicken broth over the top.
2. Cover and cook on low for 3 hours, or until the cauliflower is tender.
3. Drain any excess liquid and transfer the cauliflower to a blender or food processor.
4. Add cream cheese, butter, salt, and pepper. Blend until smooth and creamy.
5. Stir in the shredded cheddar cheese and bacon bits until well combined.
6. Transfer to a serving bowl and garnish with fresh chives.
7. Serve warm and enjoy!

Nutritional Information

Calories: 250, Protein: 10g, Carbohydrates: 8g, Fat: 20g, Fiber: 3g, Cholesterol: 50 mg, Salt: 400 mg, Potassium: 500 mg

SLOW COOKER SPAGHETTI SQUASH ALFREDO

A creamy, low-carb twist on a classic favorite, this Slow Cooker Spaghetti Squash Alfredo offers a delightful blend of flavors with minimal effort. Perfect for a comforting meal that fits your dietary needs.

Equipment

Slow Cooker, Fork, Mixing Bowl

Ingredients

- 1 kg Spaghetti Squash
- 200 ml Heavy Cream
- 100 g Grated Parmesan Cheese
- 2 cloves Garlic, minced
- 30 g Butter
- 5 g Salt
- 5 g Black Pepper
- 10 g Fresh Parsley, chopped

Directions

1. Cut the spaghetti squash in half lengthwise and remove the seeds.
2. Place the squash halves in the slow cooker, cut side down. Add 100 ml of water.
3. Cook on low for 4 hours until the squash is tender.
4. Remove the squash and use a fork to scrape out the strands into a mixing bowl.
5. In the slow cooker, combine heavy cream, Parmesan cheese, garlic, butter, salt, and pepper. Stir well.
6. Add the spaghetti squash strands back into the slow cooker and mix until well coated with the sauce.
7. Cook on low for an additional 30 minutes. Garnish with fresh parsley before serving.

Nutritional Information

Calories: 320, Protein: 8g, Carbohydrates: 12g, Fat: 28g, Fiber: 3g, Cholesterol: 80 mg, Salt: 450 mg, Potassium: 400 mg

ROASTED BELL PEPPER DIP

This creamy and flavorful roasted bell pepper dip is perfect for a low-carb snack or appetizer. The slow cooker enhances the sweetness of the peppers, creating a rich and satisfying dip.

Equipment

Slow Cooker, Blender or Food Processor, Knife

Ingredients

- 500 g Red Bell Peppers, chopped
- 200 g Cream Cheese, softened
- 100 g Greek Yogurt
- 30 ml Olive Oil
- 2 cloves Garlic, minced
- 5 g Smoked Paprika
- 5 g Salt
- 5 g Black Pepper
- 10 g Fresh Basil, chopped

Directions

1. Place the chopped red bell peppers and minced garlic in the slow cooker. Drizzle with olive oil and season with smoked paprika, salt, and black pepper.
2. Cover and cook on low for 2 hours, until the peppers are tender and aromatic.
3. Transfer the cooked peppers and garlic to a blender or food processor. Add the cream cheese and Greek yogurt.
4. Blend until smooth and creamy. Adjust seasoning if necessary.
5. Stir in the fresh basil and transfer the dip to a serving bowl.
6. Serve warm or chilled with low-carb crackers or vegetable sticks.

Nutritional Information

Calories: 120, Protein: 4g, Carbohydrates: 5g, Fat: 10g, Fiber: 2g, Cholesterol: 20mg, Salt: 300mg, Potassium: 250mg

KETO BALSAMIC MUSHROOMS

These Keto Balsamic Mushrooms are a savory delight, combining the earthy flavors of mushrooms with the tangy sweetness of balsamic vinegar, all slow-cooked to perfection.

Equipment

Slow Cooker, Mixing Bowl, Measuring Cups

Ingredients

- 500 g Button Mushrooms
- 60 ml Balsamic Vinegar
- 30 ml Olive Oil
- 2 cloves Garlic, minced
- 1 tsp Dried Thyme
- 1 tsp Salt
- 0.5 tsp Black Pepper
- 30 g Parmesan Cheese, grated (optional)

Directions

1. Clean the mushrooms and place them in the slow cooker.
2. In a mixing bowl, combine balsamic vinegar, olive oil, minced garlic, dried thyme, salt, and black pepper.
3. Pour the balsamic mixture over the mushrooms, ensuring they are well coated.
4. Cover and cook on low for 3 hours, stirring occasionally.
5. Before serving, sprinkle with grated Parmesan cheese if desired.

Nutritional Information

Calories: 120, Protein: 4g, Carbohydrates: 6g, Fat: 9g, Fiber: 2g, Cholesterol: 5 mg, Salt: 600 mg, Potassium: 400 mg

POULTRY RECIPES

SLOW COOKER BUTTER CHICKEN

Servings 4 | Prep: 15 min | Cook: 240 min

This Slow Cooker Butter Chicken is a rich and creamy dish, infused with aromatic spices, perfect for a comforting low-carb meal.

Equipment

Slow Cooker, Mixing Bowl, Measuring Cups

Ingredients

- 500 g Chicken Thighs, boneless and skinless
- 200 ml Coconut Milk
- 100 g Tomato Paste
- 50 g Onion, finely chopped
- 20 g Butter
- 10 g Garlic, minced
- 10 g Ginger, grated
- 5 g Garam Masala
- 5 g Cumin Powder
- 5 g Coriander Powder
- 2 g Turmeric Powder
- 2 g Chili Powder
- Salt, to taste
- Fresh Coriander, for garnish

Directions

1. In a mixing bowl, combine coconut milk, tomato paste, onion, garlic, ginger, garam masala, cumin, coriander, turmeric, chili powder, and salt. Mix well.
2. Place chicken thighs in the slow cooker and pour the spice mixture over the chicken, ensuring it's well-coated.
3. Add butter on top of the chicken mixture.
4. Cover and cook on low for 4 hours or until the chicken is tender and cooked through.
5. Garnish with fresh coriander before serving.

Nutritional Information

Calories: 350, Protein: 25g, Carbohydrates: 8g, Fat: 25g, Fiber: 2g, Cholesterol: 90 mg, Salt: 450 mg, Potassium: 600 mg

LEMON GARLIC CHICKEN THIGHS

Servings 4 | Prep: 10 min | Cook: 240 min

Savor the zesty and aromatic flavors of lemon and garlic infused into tender chicken thighs, all effortlessly cooked in your slow cooker. This dish is perfect for a low-carb meal that doesn't skimp on taste.

Equipment

Slow Cooker, Mixing Bowl, Measuring Spoons

Ingredients

- 800 g chicken thighs, skinless
- 60 ml lemon juice, freshly squeezed
- 4 cloves garlic, minced
- 30 ml olive oil
- 5 g dried oregano
- 5 g salt
- 2 g black pepper
- 1 lemon, sliced
- 10 g fresh parsley, chopped (for garnish)

Directions

1. In a mixing bowl, combine lemon juice, garlic, olive oil, oregano, salt, and pepper.
2. Place chicken thighs in the slow cooker and pour the lemon-garlic mixture over them.
3. Arrange lemon slices on top of the chicken.
4. Cover and cook on low for 4 hours, or until the chicken is tender and fully cooked.
5. Garnish with fresh parsley before serving.

Nutritional Information

Calories: 320, Protein: 28g, Carbohydrates: 3g, Fat: 22g, Fiber: 1g, Cholesterol: 110 mg, Salt: 600 mg, Potassium: 350 mg

KETO CHICKEN TIKKA MASALA

Servings 4 | Prep: 15 min | Cook: 240 min

This Keto Chicken Tikka Masala is a rich and creamy dish with aromatic spices, perfect for a low-carb diet. The slow cooker ensures the chicken is tender and infused with flavor.

Equipment

Slow Cooker, Mixing Bowl, Measuring Cups and Spoons

Ingredients

- 500 g Chicken Thighs, boneless and skinless
- 200 ml Coconut Milk
- 150 g Greek Yogurt
- 100 g Onion, finely chopped
- 50 g Tomato Paste
- 20 g Fresh Ginger, minced
- 10 g Garlic, minced
- 10 g Garam Masala
- 5 g Ground Cumin
- 5 g Ground Coriander
- 5 g Paprika
- 5 g Turmeric
- 5 g Salt
- 2 g Black Pepper
- 10 ml Lemon Juice
- 5 g Fresh Cilantro, chopped (for garnish)

Directions

1. In a mixing bowl, combine Greek yogurt, ginger, garlic, garam masala, cumin, coriander, paprika, turmeric, salt, pepper, and lemon juice. Mix well.
2. Add chicken thighs to the bowl, ensuring they are well-coated with the marinade. Let it marinate for at least 15 minutes.
3. Place the marinated chicken, onion, and tomato paste into the slow cooker. Stir in the coconut milk.
4. Cover and cook on low for 4 hours, or until the chicken is tender and cooked through.
5. Garnish with fresh cilantro before serving.

Nutritional Information

Calories: 350, Protein: 30g, Carbohydrates: 8g, Fat: 22g, Fiber: 2g, Cholesterol: 110 mg, Salt: 600 mg, Potassium: 650 mg

CREAMY TUSCAN CHICKEN

Servings 4 | Prep: 15 min | Cook: 240 min

This Creamy Tuscan Chicken is a delightful blend of tender chicken, sun-dried tomatoes, and spinach, all enveloped in a rich, creamy sauce. Perfect for a comforting low-carb meal.

Equipment

Slow Cooker, Mixing Bowl, Measuring Cups and Spoons

Ingredients

- 600g Chicken Breasts
- 200ml Heavy Cream
- 100g Sun-Dried Tomatoes, chopped
- 100g Fresh Spinach
- 50g Parmesan Cheese, grated
- 2 Garlic Cloves, minced
- 1 tsp Italian Seasoning
- Salt and Pepper to taste

Directions

1. Place the chicken breasts in the slow cooker.
2. In a mixing bowl, combine heavy cream, sun-dried tomatoes, garlic, Italian seasoning, salt, and pepper.
3. Pour the mixture over the chicken in the slow cooker.
4. Cook on low for 4 hours or until the chicken is tender.
5. Add spinach and Parmesan cheese, stirring until the spinach wilts and the cheese melts.
6. Serve hot, garnished with additional Parmesan if desired.

Nutritional Information

Calories: 450, Protein: 35g, Carbohydrates: 8g, Fat: 30g, Fiber: 2g, Cholesterol: 120mg, Salt: 600mg, Potassium: 750mg

GARLIC PARMESAN CHICKEN

Servings 4 | Prep: 10 min | Cook: 240 min

This Garlic Parmesan Chicken is a savory delight, combining tender chicken with the rich flavors of garlic and parmesan, all effortlessly cooked in a slow cooker.

Equipment

Slow Cooker, Mixing Bowl, Measuring Cups and Spoons

Ingredients

- 800 g chicken breasts
- 60 g parmesan cheese, grated
- 4 cloves garlic, minced
- 100 ml chicken broth
- 60 ml heavy cream
- 30 g butter
- 5 g dried oregano
- 5 g dried basil
- Salt and pepper to taste

Directions

1. Place the chicken breasts in the slow cooker.
2. In a mixing bowl, combine parmesan cheese, minced garlic, chicken broth, heavy cream, butter, oregano, basil, salt, and pepper.
3. Pour the mixture over the chicken in the slow cooker.
4. Cover and cook on low for 4 hours or until the chicken is tender and fully cooked.
5. Serve hot, garnished with additional parmesan and herbs if desired.

Nutritional Information

Calories: 350, Protein: 45g, Carbohydrates: 3g, Fat: 18g, Fiber: 0g, Cholesterol: 120 mg, Salt: 400 mg, Potassium: 600 mg

SLOW COOKER BBQ CHICKEN WINGS

Servings 4 | Prep: 10 min | Cook: 240 min

These tender, juicy chicken wings are infused with a smoky BBQ flavor, perfect for a low-carb meal that satisfies your cravings.

Equipment

Slow Cooker, Mixing Bowl, Tongs

Ingredients

- 1 kg Chicken Wings
- 200 ml Sugar-Free BBQ Sauce
- 1 tbsp Paprika
- 1 tsp Garlic Powder
- 1 tsp Onion Powder
- 1 tsp Salt
- 1/2 tsp Black Pepper

Directions

1. In a mixing bowl, combine the BBQ sauce, paprika, garlic powder, onion powder, salt, and black pepper.
2. Place the chicken wings in the slow cooker and pour the BBQ sauce mixture over them, ensuring they are well coated.
3. Cover and cook on low for 4 hours or until the wings are tender and cooked through.
4. Use tongs to remove the wings from the slow cooker and serve hot.

Nutritional Information

Calories: 320, Protein: 25g, Carbohydrates: 5g, Fat: 22g, Fiber: 1g, Cholesterol: 110 mg, Salt: 600 mg, Potassium: 350 mg

THAI COCONUT CHICKEN CURRY

This Thai Coconut Chicken Curry is a delightful blend of creamy coconut milk, tender chicken, and aromatic spices, all simmered to perfection in a slow cooker. It's a comforting, low-carb dish that brings the exotic flavors of Thailand to your table with minimal effort.

Equipment

Slow Cooker, Cutting Board, Knife

Ingredients

- 500 g Chicken Thighs, boneless and skinless
- 400 ml Coconut Milk
- 200 g Bell Peppers, sliced
- 100 g Onion, chopped
- 30 g Red Curry Paste
- 10 g Fresh Ginger, minced
- 5 g Garlic, minced
- 15 ml Fish Sauce
- 10 ml Lime Juice
- 5 g Fresh Basil, chopped

Directions

1. Place the chicken thighs at the bottom of the slow cooker.
2. In a bowl, mix coconut milk, red curry paste, ginger, garlic, and fish sauce until well combined.
3. Pour the coconut milk mixture over the chicken in the slow cooker.
4. Add sliced bell peppers and chopped onion on top.
5. Cover and cook on low for 4 hours, or until the chicken is tender.
6. Stir in lime juice and fresh basil before serving.

Nutritional Information

Calories: 350, Protein: 25g, Carbohydrates: 10g, Fat: 25g, Fiber: 3g, Cholesterol: 70 mg, Salt: 600 mg, Potassium: 450 mg

HERB-CRUSTED TURKEY BREAST

This herb-crusted turkey breast is a succulent and flavorful dish, perfect for a low-carb meal. The slow cooker ensures the turkey remains juicy and tender, while the herb crust adds a delightful aromatic touch.

Equipment

Slow Cooker, Mixing Bowl, Measuring Spoons

Ingredients

- 1.5 kg Turkey Breast
- 30 g Fresh Parsley, chopped
- 15 g Fresh Thyme, chopped
- 15 g Fresh Rosemary, chopped
- 4 cloves Garlic, minced
- 60 ml Olive Oil
- 5 g Salt
- 3 g Black Pepper

Directions

1. In a mixing bowl, combine parsley, thyme, rosemary, garlic, olive oil, salt, and pepper to form a paste.
2. Rub the herb mixture evenly over the turkey breast.
3. Place the turkey breast in the slow cooker.
4. Cover and cook on low for 4 hours, or until the internal temperature reaches 75°C.
5. Let the turkey rest for 10 minutes before slicing and serving.

Nutritional Information

Calories: 320, Protein: 45g, Carbohydrates: 2g, Fat: 15g, Fiber: 0g, Cholesterol: 110 mg, Salt: 400 mg, Potassium: 550 mg

CHEESY BUFFALO CHICKEN DIP

Servings 8 | Prep: 10 min | Cook: 180 min

This creamy, spicy, and cheesy dip is perfect for gatherings or a cozy night in. The slow cooker melds the flavors beautifully, making it a crowd-pleaser with minimal effort.

Equipment

Slow Cooker, Mixing Bowl, Spoon

Ingredients

- 500 g boneless, skinless chicken breasts
- 250 g cream cheese, softened
- 120 ml hot sauce
- 100 g shredded cheddar cheese
- 100 g shredded mozzarella cheese
- 60 ml ranch dressing
- 1 tsp garlic powder
- 1 tsp onion powder

Directions

1. Place the chicken breasts in the slow cooker.
2. In a mixing bowl, combine cream cheese, hot sauce, ranch dressing, garlic powder, and onion powder. Mix until smooth.
3. Pour the mixture over the chicken in the slow cooker.
4. Cook on low for 3 hours or until the chicken is fully cooked and tender.
5. Shred the chicken using two forks, then stir in the cheddar and mozzarella cheeses.
6. Allow the dip to cook for an additional 15 minutes, until the cheese is melted and bubbly.
7. Serve warm with low-carb veggies or keto-friendly chips.

Nutritional Information

Calories: 250, Protein: 20g, Carbohydrates: 3g, Fat: 18g, Fiber: 0g, Cholesterol: 80 mg, Salt: 600 mg, Potassium: 250 mg

LOW CARB TERIYAKI CHICKEN

Servings 4 | Prep: 10 min | Cook: 240 min

This low carb teriyaki chicken is a savory and slightly sweet dish, perfect for a healthy and satisfying meal. The slow cooker ensures the chicken is tender and infused with rich flavors.

Equipment

Slow Cooker, Mixing Bowl, Whisk

Ingredients

- 600g Chicken Thighs, boneless and skinless
- 100ml Soy Sauce, low sodium
- 60ml Water
- 30ml Rice Vinegar
- 2g Garlic Powder
- 2g Ginger Powder
- 5g Sesame Seeds
- 5g Green Onions, chopped

Directions

1. In a mixing bowl, whisk together soy sauce, water, rice vinegar, garlic powder, and ginger powder.
2. Place the chicken thighs in the slow cooker and pour the sauce mixture over them.
3. Cover and cook on low for 4 hours, or until the chicken is tender and fully cooked.
4. Once cooked, remove the chicken and shred it using two forks.
5. Return the shredded chicken to the slow cooker and stir to coat with the sauce.
6. Serve hot, garnished with sesame seeds and chopped green onions.

Nutritional Information

Calories: 250, Protein: 30g, Carbohydrates: 4g, Fat: 12g, Fiber: 1g, Cholesterol: 110mg, Salt: 800mg, Potassium: 450mg

CHICKEN FAJITA CASSEROLE

Servings 4 | Prep: 15 min | Cook: 240 min

This Chicken Fajita Casserole combines the vibrant flavors of fajitas with the convenience of a slow cooker, offering a delicious low-carb meal that's both satisfying and easy to prepare.

Equipment

Slow Cooker, Cutting Board, Knife

Ingredients

- 500 g Chicken Breast, sliced
- 1 Red Bell Pepper, sliced
- 1 Green Bell Pepper, sliced
- 1 Yellow Onion, sliced
- 200 g Canned Diced Tomatoes
- 100 g Cheddar Cheese, shredded
- 2 cloves Garlic, minced
- 10 g Fajita Seasoning
- 30 ml Olive Oil
- Salt and Pepper to taste

Directions

1. In a slow cooker, combine chicken, bell peppers, onion, diced tomatoes, and garlic.
2. Sprinkle fajita seasoning over the mixture and drizzle with olive oil. Stir to combine.
3. Cover and cook on low for 4 hours, or until the chicken is cooked through and tender.
4. About 15 minutes before serving, sprinkle shredded cheddar cheese over the top and allow it to melt.
5. Season with salt and pepper to taste before serving.

Nutritional Information

Calories: 320, Protein: 35g, Carbohydrates: 10g, Fat: 15g, Fiber: 3g, Cholesterol: 85 mg, Salt: 450 mg, Potassium: 750 mg

SPINACH & CHEESE STUFFED CHICKEN

Servings 4 | Prep: 15 min | Cook: 240 min

This delightful dish features tender chicken breasts stuffed with a creamy spinach and cheese mixture, all cooked to perfection in a slow cooker. It's a low-carb, high-flavor meal that's sure to impress.

Equipment

Slow Cooker, Mixing Bowl, Knife, Cutting Board

Ingredients

- 4 large chicken breasts (approximately 800g)
- 150g fresh spinach, chopped
- 100g cream cheese, softened
- 100g mozzarella cheese, shredded
- 2 cloves garlic, minced
- 15ml olive oil
- 5g salt
- 3g black pepper
- 5g paprika

Directions

1. In a mixing bowl, combine the chopped spinach, cream cheese, mozzarella, and minced garlic. Mix until well blended.
2. Carefully cut a pocket into each chicken breast, being cautious not to cut all the way through.
3. Stuff each chicken breast with the spinach and cheese mixture, then secure with toothpicks if necessary.
4. Rub the outside of the chicken breasts with olive oil, salt, pepper, and paprika.
5. Place the stuffed chicken breasts in the slow cooker, cover, and cook on low for 4 hours or until the chicken is fully cooked and tender.

Nutritional Information

Calories: 380, Protein: 45g, Carbohydrates: 4g, Fat: 20g, Fiber: 1g, Cholesterol: 120mg, Salt: 600mg, Potassium: 750mg

CREAMY PESTO CHICKEN

Servings 4 | Prep: 10 min | Cook: 240 min

This creamy pesto chicken is a delightful low-carb dish that combines tender chicken with the rich flavors of basil pesto and cream. Perfect for a comforting meal any day of the week.

Equipment

Slow Cooker, Mixing Bowl, Measuring Cups and Spoons

Ingredients

- 800 g Chicken Breasts
- 150 g Basil Pesto
- 200 ml Heavy Cream
- 100 g Cherry Tomatoes, halved
- 50 g Parmesan Cheese, grated
- 2 cloves Garlic, minced
- Salt and Pepper to taste

Directions

1. Place the chicken breasts in the slow cooker.
2. In a mixing bowl, combine the basil pesto, heavy cream, and minced garlic. Mix well.
3. Pour the pesto mixture over the chicken, ensuring all pieces are well coated.
4. Add the cherry tomatoes to the slow cooker.
5. Cover and cook on low for 4 hours or until the chicken is tender.
6. Before serving, sprinkle grated Parmesan cheese over the chicken.
7. Season with salt and pepper to taste.

Nutritional Information

Calories: 450, Protein: 35g, Carbohydrates: 5g, Fat: 32g, Fiber: 1g, Cholesterol: 120 mg, Salt: 450 mg, Potassium: 600 mg

GREEK SLOW COOKER CHICKEN

Servings 4 | Prep: 15 min | Cook: 240 min

Experience the vibrant flavors of Greece with this succulent slow-cooked chicken, infused with herbs and lemon for a refreshing low-carb delight.

Equipment

Slow Cooker, Mixing Bowl, Measuring Cups

Ingredients

- 800 g Chicken Thighs, skinless
- 100 ml Olive Oil
- 60 ml Lemon Juice
- 4 cloves Garlic, minced
- 10 g Dried Oregano
- 5 g Dried Thyme
- 5 g Salt
- 3 g Black Pepper
- 100 g Kalamata Olives, pitted
- 150 g Cherry Tomatoes, halved
- 1 Red Onion, sliced

Directions

1. In a mixing bowl, combine olive oil, lemon juice, garlic, oregano, thyme, salt, and pepper.
2. Place chicken thighs in the slow cooker and pour the olive oil mixture over them, ensuring even coating.
3. Add kalamata olives, cherry tomatoes, and red onion on top of the chicken.
4. Cover and cook on low for 4 hours, or until the chicken is tender and fully cooked.
5. Serve hot, garnished with fresh herbs if desired.

Nutritional Information

Calories: 450, Protein: 35g, Carbohydrates: 8g, Fat: 30g, Fiber: 2g, Cholesterol: 120 mg, Salt: 600 mg, Potassium: 500 mg

KETO RANCH CHICKEN

Savor the creamy and tangy flavors of ranch-infused chicken, perfect for a low-carb lifestyle. This dish is effortlessly prepared in a slow cooker, making it a convenient and delicious meal for any day of the week.

Equipment

Slow Cooker, Mixing Bowl, Measuring Cups and Spoons

Ingredients

- 800 g Chicken Breasts
- 250 ml Heavy Cream
- 60 g Cream Cheese
- 30 g Ranch Seasoning Mix
- 100 g Bacon, cooked and crumbled
- 50 g Cheddar Cheese, shredded
- 10 g Fresh Parsley, chopped

Directions

1. Place the chicken breasts in the slow cooker.
2. In a mixing bowl, combine the heavy cream, cream cheese, and ranch seasoning mix. Stir until smooth.
3. Pour the cream mixture over the chicken in the slow cooker.
4. Cover and cook on low for 4 hours, or until the chicken is tender and cooked through.
5. Once cooked, shred the chicken with two forks and mix it well with the sauce.
6. Stir in the crumbled bacon and shredded cheddar cheese.
7. Garnish with fresh parsley before serving.

Nutritional Information

Calories: 520, Protein: 45g, Carbohydrates: 5g, Fat: 35g, Fiber: 1g, Cholesterol: 150 mg, Salt: 850 mg, Potassium: 750 mg

CHICKEN ALFREDO SOUP

A creamy, comforting low-carb soup that combines the rich flavors of Alfredo sauce with tender chicken, perfect for a cozy meal.

Equipment

Slow Cooker, Cutting Board, Knife

Ingredients

- 500 g Chicken Breast, diced
- 200 g Cream Cheese, cubed
- 500 ml Chicken Broth
- 100 g Parmesan Cheese, grated
- 150 ml Heavy Cream
- 100 g Spinach, fresh
- 3 cloves Garlic, minced
- 1 tsp Salt
- 1/2 tsp Black Pepper

Directions

1. Place the diced chicken breast in the slow cooker.
2. Add cream cheese, chicken broth, Parmesan cheese, heavy cream, garlic, salt, and black pepper.
3. Stir to combine all ingredients well.
4. Cover and cook on low for 4 hours, or until the chicken is cooked through and tender.
5. About 30 minutes before serving, add the fresh spinach and stir until wilted.
6. Adjust seasoning if necessary and serve hot.

Nutritional Information

Calories: 350, Protein: 30g, Carbohydrates: 5g, Fat: 24g, Fiber: 1g, Cholesterol: 110 mg, Salt: 800 mg, Potassium: 450 mg

SLOW COOKER MOROCCAN CHICKEN

Servings 4 | Prep: 15 min | Cook: 240 min

This Moroccan Chicken is a delightful blend of spices and tender chicken, slow-cooked to perfection. The aromatic flavors will transport you to the bustling markets of Marrakech.

Equipment

Slow Cooker, Mixing Bowl, Measuring Spoons

Ingredients

- 800 g chicken thighs, skinless and boneless
- 200 g canned tomatoes, diced
- 100 g onion, chopped
- 2 cloves garlic, minced
- 50 g green olives, pitted and sliced
- 30 ml olive oil
- 15 g ground cumin
- 10 g ground coriander
- 5 g ground cinnamon
- 5 g paprika
- 5 g salt
- 2 g black pepper
- 1 g saffron threads
- 100 ml chicken broth
- 30 g fresh cilantro, chopped

Directions

1. In a mixing bowl, combine cumin, coriander, cinnamon, paprika, salt, and pepper. Rub the spice mixture over the chicken thighs.
2. Heat olive oil in a pan over medium heat. Sear the chicken thighs until browned on both sides, about 3-4 minutes per side.
3. Transfer the chicken to the slow cooker. Add onions, garlic, tomatoes, olives, and saffron threads.
4. Pour chicken broth over the mixture. Cover and cook on low for 4 hours, or until the chicken is tender.
5. Garnish with fresh cilantro before serving.

Nutritional Information

Calories: 350, Protein: 30g, Carbohydrates: 10g, Fat: 20g, Fiber: 3g, Cholesterol: 110 mg, Salt: 600 mg, Potassium: 500 mg

GARLIC BUTTER ROAST DUCK

Servings 4 | Prep: 15 min | Cook: 240 min

Indulge in the rich flavors of tender duck infused with aromatic garlic and creamy butter, all effortlessly cooked to perfection in your slow cooker.

Equipment

Slow Cooker, Mixing Bowl, Basting Brush

Ingredients

- 1.5 kg Whole Duck
- 100 g Unsalted Butter, softened
- 10 cloves Garlic, minced
- 10 g Fresh Thyme
- 5 g Salt
- 5 g Black Pepper
- 50 ml Lemon Juice

Directions

1. Pat the duck dry with paper towels and season the cavity with salt and pepper.
2. In a mixing bowl, combine the softened butter, minced garlic, fresh thyme, salt, and pepper.
3. Rub the garlic butter mixture generously over the entire duck, ensuring even coverage.
4. Place the duck in the slow cooker and drizzle with lemon juice.
5. Cover and cook on low for 4 hours, or until the duck is tender and fully cooked.
6. For a crispy skin, transfer the duck to an oven-safe dish and broil for 5 minutes.
7. Let the duck rest for 10 minutes before carving and serving.

Nutritional Information

Calories: 620, Protein: 45g, Carbohydrates: 2g, Fat: 48g, Fiber: 0g, Cholesterol: 220 mg, Salt: 600 mg, Potassium: 450 mg

SLOW COOKER JERK CHICKEN

Servings 4 | Prep: 15 min | Cook: 240 min

Dive into the vibrant flavors of the Caribbean with this Slow Cooker Jerk Chicken. It's a perfect blend of spices and tender chicken, all cooked to perfection in your slow cooker.

Equipment

Slow Cooker, Mixing Bowl, Measuring Spoons

Ingredients

- 800 g Chicken Thighs, skinless
- 50 ml Lime Juice
- 30 g Jerk Seasoning
- 2 cloves Garlic, minced
- 1 Onion, sliced
- 1 Red Bell Pepper, sliced
- 200 ml Chicken Broth

Directions

1. In a mixing bowl, combine lime juice, jerk seasoning, and minced garlic.
2. Rub the mixture over the chicken thighs, ensuring they are well coated.
3. Place the onion and red bell pepper at the bottom of the slow cooker.
4. Add the seasoned chicken thighs on top of the vegetables.
5. Pour the chicken broth over the chicken and vegetables.
6. Cover and cook on low for 4 hours, or until the chicken is tender and cooked through.
7. Serve hot, garnished with fresh herbs if desired.

Nutritional Information

Calories: 320, Protein: 35g, Carbohydrates: 8g, Fat: 18g, Fiber: 2g, Cholesterol: 120 mg, Salt: 600 mg, Potassium: 450 mg

KETO CHICKEN FLORENTINE

Servings 4 | Prep: 15 min | Cook: 240 min

This Keto Chicken Florentine is a creamy, flavorful dish that combines tender chicken with spinach and a rich, cheesy sauce, all cooked to perfection in a slow cooker.

Equipment

Slow Cooker, Mixing Bowl, Whisk

Ingredients

- 600 g Chicken Breasts
- 200 g Fresh Spinach
- 150 g Cream Cheese
- 100 ml Heavy Cream
- 100 g Parmesan Cheese, grated
- 2 cloves Garlic, minced
- 1 tsp Salt
- 1/2 tsp Black Pepper
- 1/2 tsp Nutmeg

Directions

1. Place the chicken breasts in the slow cooker.
2. In a mixing bowl, combine cream cheese, heavy cream, Parmesan cheese, garlic, salt, pepper, and nutmeg. Whisk until smooth.
3. Pour the cheese mixture over the chicken in the slow cooker.
4. Add the fresh spinach on top of the chicken and cheese mixture.
5. Cover and cook on low for 4 hours, or until the chicken is tender and fully cooked.
6. Stir the mixture gently to combine the spinach with the sauce before serving.

Nutritional Information

Calories: 420, Protein: 38g, Carbohydrates: 5g, Fat: 28g, Fiber: 2g, Cholesterol: 110 mg, Salt: 700 mg, Potassium: 750 mg

SEAFOOD

LEMON BUTTER GARLIC SALMON

Servings 4 | Prep: 10 min | Cook: 120 min

This dish combines the rich flavors of salmon with the zesty brightness of lemon and the savory depth of garlic, all slow-cooked to perfection in a buttery sauce.

Equipment

Slow Cooker, Mixing Bowl, Whisk

Ingredients

- 600 g Salmon Fillets
- 50 g Unsalted Butter, melted
- 3 cloves Garlic, minced
- 60 ml Fresh Lemon Juice
- 1 Lemon, sliced
- 5 g Fresh Dill, chopped
- Salt and Pepper to taste

Directions

1. In a mixing bowl, whisk together the melted butter, minced garlic, and fresh lemon juice.
2. Season the salmon fillets with salt and pepper, then place them in the slow cooker.
3. Pour the lemon butter garlic mixture over the salmon fillets.
4. Layer the lemon slices on top of the salmon.
5. Cover and cook on low for 2 hours, or until the salmon is cooked through and flakes easily with a fork.
6. Garnish with fresh dill before serving.

Nutritional Information

Calories: 320, Protein: 34g, Carbohydrates: 2g, Fat: 20g, Fiber: 0g, Cholesterol: 95 mg, Salt: 300 mg, Potassium: 750 mg

SLOW COOKER SHRIMP SCAMPI

Servings 4 | Prep: 10 min | Cook: 120 min

This low-carb shrimp scampi is a delightful blend of succulent shrimp, garlic, and lemon, all slow-cooked to perfection. It's a simple yet elegant dish that brings the flavors of the sea to your table with minimal effort.

Equipment

Slow Cooker, Mixing Bowl, Measuring Cups and Spoons

Ingredients

- 500 g shrimp, peeled and deveined
- 60 ml olive oil
- 4 cloves garlic, minced
- 60 ml chicken broth
- 30 ml lemon juice
- 1 tsp dried parsley
- 1/2 tsp red pepper flakes
- Salt and pepper to taste

Directions

1. In a mixing bowl, combine olive oil, garlic, chicken broth, lemon juice, dried parsley, red pepper flakes, salt, and pepper.
2. Place the shrimp in the slow cooker and pour the mixture over the shrimp, ensuring they are well-coated.
3. Cover and cook on low for 2 hours or until the shrimp are cooked through and tender.
4. Stir occasionally to ensure even cooking and flavor distribution.
5. Serve hot, garnished with additional parsley if desired.

Nutritional Information

Calories: 220, Protein: 25g, Carbohydrates: 3g, Fat: 12g, Fiber: 0g, Cholesterol: 190 mg, Salt: 400 mg, Potassium: 300 mg

KETO CLAM CHOWDER

Indulge in a creamy, rich, and satisfying Keto Clam Chowder that brings the taste of the sea to your table without the carbs. Perfect for a cozy meal, this chowder is a delightful blend of clams, vegetables, and spices, all simmered to perfection in your slow cooker.

Equipment

Slow Cooker, Knife, Cutting Board

Ingredients

- 500 g clams, cleaned
- 200 g cauliflower, chopped
- 100 g celery, diced
- 100 g onion, diced
- 200 ml heavy cream
- 500 ml chicken broth
- 2 cloves garlic, minced
- 30 g butter
- 5 g thyme, fresh
- Salt and pepper to taste

Directions

1. In the slow cooker, combine clams, cauliflower, celery, onion, garlic, and thyme.
2. Pour in the chicken broth and add butter. Stir to combine.
3. Cover and cook on low for 4 hours, until vegetables are tender.
4. Stir in heavy cream and season with salt and pepper.
5. Cook for an additional 30 minutes on low to heat through.
6. Serve hot, garnished with fresh thyme if desired.

Nutritional Information

Calories: 320, Protein: 18g, Carbohydrates: 8g, Fat: 24g, Fiber: 2g, Cholesterol: 90 mg, Salt: 600 mg, Potassium: 450 mg

CAJUN-STYLE SLOW COOKER TILAPIA

This Cajun-Style Slow Cooker Tilapia is a flavorful and easy-to-make dish, perfect for a low-carb diet. The blend of spices and tender fish creates a delightful meal with minimal effort.

Equipment

Slow Cooker, Mixing Bowl, Measuring Spoons

Ingredients

- 600 g Tilapia fillets
- 30 ml Olive oil
- 10 g Cajun seasoning
- 5 g Garlic powder
- 5 g Onion powder
- 2 g Paprika
- 1 g Black pepper
- 1 g Salt
- 1 Lemon, sliced
- 100 g Bell peppers, sliced
- 100 g Cherry tomatoes, halved

Directions

1. In a mixing bowl, combine olive oil, Cajun seasoning, garlic powder, onion powder, paprika, black pepper, and salt.
2. Rub the spice mixture evenly over the tilapia fillets.
3. Place the seasoned tilapia in the slow cooker, layering with lemon slices, bell peppers, and cherry tomatoes.
4. Cover and cook on low for 3 hours, or until the fish flakes easily with a fork.
5. Serve warm, garnished with additional lemon slices if desired.

Nutritional Information

Calories: 220, Protein: 30g, Carbohydrates: 5g, Fat: 10g, Fiber: 2g, Cholesterol: 60 mg, Salt: 400 mg, Potassium: 600 mg

GARLIC BUTTER LOBSTER TAILS

Servings 4 | Prep: 10 min | Cook: 60 min

Indulge in the luxurious taste of tender lobster tails bathed in a rich garlic butter sauce, all effortlessly prepared in your slow cooker. Perfect for a special occasion or a delightful dinner treat.

Equipment

Slow Cooker, Small Saucepan, Basting Brush

Ingredients

- 4 lobster tails (approximately 200g each)
- 100g unsalted butter
- 4 cloves garlic, minced
- 30ml lemon juice
- 5g fresh parsley, chopped
- 5g salt
- 2g black pepper

Directions

1. In a small saucepan, melt the butter over low heat. Add minced garlic and sauté until fragrant, about 2 minutes.
2. Stir in lemon juice, salt, and black pepper. Remove from heat and set aside.
3. Using kitchen shears, cut the top shell of each lobster tail down to the tail fin. Gently pull apart the shell to expose the meat.
4. Place lobster tails in the slow cooker. Brush generously with the garlic butter sauce, ensuring the meat is well-coated.
5. Cover and cook on low for 60 minutes, or until the lobster meat is opaque and tender.
6. Garnish with fresh parsley before serving.

Nutritional Information

Calories: 320, Protein: 28g, Carbohydrates: 2g, Fat: 22g, Fiber: 0g, Cholesterol: 150mg, Salt: 480mg, Potassium: 250mg

SLOW COOKER TUNA STEAK

Servings 4 | Prep: 10 min | Cook: 120 min

This slow cooker tuna steak recipe is a delightful low-carb seafood dish, perfect for a healthy and flavorful meal. The tuna is infused with aromatic herbs and spices, making it tender and delicious.

Equipment

Slow Cooker, Mixing Bowl, Measuring Cups and Spoons

Ingredients

- 600 g Tuna Steaks
- 30 ml Olive Oil
- 2 cloves Garlic, minced
- 5 g Fresh Thyme, chopped
- 5 g Fresh Rosemary, chopped
- 60 ml Lemon Juice
- 5 g Salt
- 3 g Black Pepper
- 100 g Cherry Tomatoes, halved
- 50 g Black Olives, pitted and sliced

Directions

1. In a mixing bowl, combine olive oil, garlic, thyme, rosemary, lemon juice, salt, and black pepper.
2. Place tuna steaks in the slow cooker and pour the olive oil mixture over them, ensuring they are well coated.
3. Add cherry tomatoes and black olives around the tuna steaks.
4. Cover the slow cooker and cook on low for 2 hours or until the tuna is cooked through and tender.
5. Serve the tuna steaks with the cooked tomatoes and olives, drizzling any remaining sauce over the top.

Nutritional Information

Calories: 320, Protein: 40g, Carbohydrates: 5g, Fat: 16g, Fiber: 2g, Cholesterol: 70 mg, Salt: 600 mg, Potassium: 750 mg

THAI COCONUT CURRY SHRIMP

Servings 4 | Prep: 15 min | Cook: 180 min

Experience the exotic flavors of Thailand with this creamy, aromatic coconut curry shrimp dish. Perfectly cooked in a slow cooker, this low-carb meal is both satisfying and easy to prepare.

Equipment

Slow Cooker, Mixing Bowl, Measuring Cups

Ingredients

- 500 g Shrimp, peeled and deveined
- 400 ml Coconut Milk
- 150 g Red Bell Pepper, sliced
- 100 g Onion, chopped
- 2 cloves Garlic, minced
- 30 g Red Curry Paste
- 10 g Fresh Ginger, grated
- 15 ml Fish Sauce
- 10 ml Lime Juice
- 5 g Fresh Basil, chopped

Directions

1. In a mixing bowl, combine coconut milk, red curry paste, fish sauce, lime juice, garlic, and ginger. Mix well.
2. Place shrimp, red bell pepper, and onion in the slow cooker.
3. Pour the coconut milk mixture over the shrimp and vegetables. Stir to combine.
4. Cover and cook on low for 3 hours, or until shrimp are cooked through and vegetables are tender.
5. Stir in fresh basil before serving.

Nutritional Information

Calories: 320, Protein: 25g, Carbohydrates: 10g, Fat: 20g, Fiber: 2g, Cholesterol: 180 mg, Salt: 600 mg, Potassium: 450 mg

SMOKED PAPRIKA SALMON STEW

Servings 4 | Prep: 15 min | Cook: 240 min

This hearty and flavorful salmon stew, infused with smoked paprika, is a perfect low-carb meal that brings warmth and comfort with every bite.

Equipment

Slow Cooker, Cutting Board, Knife

Ingredients

- 600 g salmon fillets, skin removed and cut into chunks
- 1 medium onion, chopped
- 2 cloves garlic, minced
- 400 g canned tomatoes, diced
- 200 ml fish stock
- 1 red bell pepper, sliced
- 1 tsp smoked paprika
- 1 tsp salt
- 1/2 tsp black pepper
- 1 tbsp olive oil
- 1 tbsp fresh parsley, chopped

Directions

1. Heat olive oil in a pan over medium heat and sauté onion and garlic until translucent.
2. Transfer the onion and garlic to the slow cooker. Add salmon, canned tomatoes, fish stock, red bell pepper, smoked paprika, salt, and black pepper.
3. Stir gently to combine all ingredients.
4. Cover and cook on low for 4 hours, or until the salmon is cooked through and the flavors meld together.
5. Garnish with fresh parsley before serving.

Nutritional Information

Calories: 320, Protein: 35g, Carbohydrates: 10g, Fat: 15g, Fiber: 3g, Cholesterol: 85 mg, Salt: 600 mg, Potassium: 950 mg

KETO FISH CHOWDER

A creamy, hearty chowder that brings the rich flavors of the sea to your table, all while keeping it low-carb and keto-friendly.

Equipment

Slow Cooker, Knife, Cutting Board

Ingredients

- 500 g white fish fillets, cut into chunks
- 200 g cauliflower florets
- 150 g celery, chopped
- 100 g onion, diced
- 2 cloves garlic, minced
- 500 ml fish stock
- 200 ml heavy cream
- 30 g butter
- 5 g fresh thyme
- Salt and pepper to taste

Directions

1. Place the fish, cauliflower, celery, onion, and garlic into the slow cooker.
2. Pour in the fish stock and add the butter, thyme, salt, and pepper.
3. Cover and cook on low for 4 hours.
4. Stir in the heavy cream and adjust seasoning if needed.
5. Cook for an additional 30 minutes on low.
6. Serve hot, garnished with fresh thyme if desired.

Nutritional Information

Calories: 320, Protein: 25g, Carbohydrates: 8g, Fat: 22g, Fiber: 3g, Cholesterol: 85 mg, Salt: 450 mg, Potassium: 750 mg

SLOW COOKER CRAB CAKES

Delight in these tender and flavorful crab cakes, perfectly cooked in a slow cooker to maintain their delicate texture and rich taste. A low-carb twist on a classic favorite, ideal for seafood lovers seeking a healthier option.

Equipment

Slow Cooker, Mixing Bowl, Spatula

Ingredients

- 500 g fresh crab meat
- 100 g almond flour
- 1 large egg
- 50 ml mayonnaise
- 10 ml Dijon mustard
- 5 g garlic powder
- 5 g onion powder
- 5 g paprika
- 2 g salt
- 2 g black pepper
- 15 ml lemon juice
- 10 g fresh parsley, chopped

Directions

1. In a mixing bowl, combine crab meat, almond flour, egg, mayonnaise, Dijon mustard, garlic powder, onion powder, paprika, salt, and black pepper. Mix gently until well combined.
2. Shape the mixture into 8 small patties.
3. Line the bottom of the slow cooker with parchment paper to prevent sticking.
4. Place the crab cakes in a single layer in the slow cooker.
5. Cover and cook on low for 2 hours, or until the crab cakes are firm and cooked through.
6. Carefully remove the crab cakes using a spatula and drizzle with lemon juice.
7. Garnish with fresh parsley before serving.

Nutritional Information

Calories: 220, Protein: 25g, Carbohydrates: 5g, Fat: 12g, Fiber: 2g, Cholesterol: 95 mg, Salt: 300 mg, Potassium: 250 mg

GARLIC PARMESAN COD FILLETS

Savor the delicate flavors of cod fillets infused with garlic and Parmesan, all cooked to perfection in a slow cooker for a low-carb delight.

Equipment

Slow Cooker, Mixing Bowl, Measuring Cups

Ingredients

- 600 g Cod Fillets
- 50 g Parmesan Cheese, grated
- 30 ml Olive Oil
- 4 cloves Garlic, minced
- 10 g Fresh Parsley, chopped
- 5 g Salt
- 2 g Black Pepper
- 15 ml Lemon Juice

Directions

1. In a mixing bowl, combine Parmesan cheese, olive oil, minced garlic, chopped parsley, salt, and black pepper.
2. Place the cod fillets in the slow cooker and drizzle with lemon juice.
3. Spread the Parmesan mixture evenly over the cod fillets.
4. Cover and cook on low for 2 hours, or until the fish flakes easily with a fork.
5. Serve warm, garnished with additional parsley if desired.

Nutritional Information

Calories: 250, Protein: 35g, Carbohydrates: 2g, Fat: 12g, Fiber: 0g, Cholesterol: 80 mg, Salt: 500 mg, Potassium: 750 mg

MISO GLAZED SALMON

This Miso Glazed Salmon is a delightful blend of savory and sweet, with a rich umami flavor that pairs perfectly with the tender, flaky salmon. It's a simple yet elegant dish that brings out the best in seafood.

Equipment

Slow Cooker, Mixing Bowl, Whisk

Ingredients

- 600 g Salmon Fillets
- 60 ml Miso Paste
- 30 ml Soy Sauce
- 30 ml Rice Vinegar
- 15 ml Sesame Oil
- 10 g Fresh Ginger, grated
- 2 Garlic Cloves, minced
- 5 g Sesame Seeds, for garnish
- 10 g Spring Onions, chopped, for garnish

Directions

1. In a mixing bowl, whisk together the miso paste, soy sauce, rice vinegar, sesame oil, ginger, and garlic until smooth.
2. Place the salmon fillets in the slow cooker and pour the miso mixture over them, ensuring they are well coated.
3. Cover and cook on low for 2 hours, or until the salmon is cooked through and flakes easily with a fork.
4. Once cooked, carefully remove the salmon from the slow cooker and place it on a serving platter.
5. Garnish with sesame seeds and chopped spring onions before serving.

Nutritional Information

Calories: 320, Protein: 35g, Carbohydrates: 5g, Fat: 18g, Fiber: 1g, Cholesterol: 85 mg, Salt: 720 mg, Potassium: 750 mg

SPICY SHRIMP AND CHORIZO

Servings 4 | Prep: 15 min | Cook: 180 min

This dish combines succulent shrimp with spicy chorizo, creating a flavorful and satisfying low-carb meal. Perfect for a cozy dinner, it brings a touch of spice and warmth to your table.

Equipment

Slow Cooker, Skillet, Mixing Bowl

Ingredients

- 500 g shrimp, peeled and deveined
- 200 g chorizo, sliced
- 1 red bell pepper, sliced
- 1 green bell pepper, sliced
- 1 onion, chopped
- 3 cloves garlic, minced
- 200 ml chicken broth
- 1 tsp smoked paprika
- 1/2 tsp cayenne pepper
- Salt and pepper to taste
- 2 tbsp olive oil
- 1 tbsp fresh parsley, chopped (for garnish)

Directions

1. Heat olive oil in a skillet over medium heat. Add chorizo slices and cook until browned. Remove and set aside.
2. In the same skillet, add onion, garlic, and bell peppers. Sauté until softened.
3. Transfer the sautéed vegetables and chorizo to the slow cooker. Add shrimp, chicken broth, smoked paprika, cayenne pepper, salt, and pepper.
4. Stir to combine all ingredients. Cover and cook on low for 3 hours.
5. Before serving, garnish with fresh parsley.

Nutritional Information

Calories: 320, Protein: 28g, Carbohydrates: 8g, Fat: 20g, Fiber: 2g, Cholesterol: 190 mg, Salt: 850 mg, Potassium: 550 mg

SLOW COOKER HALIBUT STEW

Servings 4 | Prep: 15 min | Cook: 240 min

This hearty and flavorful halibut stew is a perfect low-carb meal, combining tender fish with a medley of vegetables and spices, all simmered to perfection in a slow cooker.

Equipment

Slow Cooker, Cutting Board, Knife

Ingredients

- 600 g Halibut fillets, cut into chunks
- 200 g Zucchini, sliced
- 150 g Bell peppers, chopped
- 100 g Onion, diced
- 400 g Canned tomatoes, diced
- 500 ml Fish stock
- 2 cloves Garlic, minced
- 10 g Fresh parsley, chopped
- 5 g Dried thyme
- 5 g Paprika
- Salt and pepper to taste

Directions

1. Place the halibut chunks in the slow cooker.
2. Add zucchini, bell peppers, onion, and canned tomatoes over the fish.
3. Pour in the fish stock and add garlic, parsley, thyme, and paprika.
4. Season with salt and pepper to taste.
5. Cover and cook on low for 4 hours, until the fish is tender and flavors meld.
6. Stir gently before serving to combine the ingredients.

Nutritional Information

Calories: 250, Protein: 30g, Carbohydrates: 12g, Fat: 8g, Fiber: 3g, Cholesterol: 60 mg, Salt: 500 mg, Potassium: 900 mg

KETO SEAFOOD GUMBO

Dive into the rich and flavorful world of Keto Seafood Gumbo, a low-carb delight that brings the essence of the sea to your slow cooker. Perfectly seasoned and packed with protein, this dish is a comforting and satisfying meal for any seafood lover.

Equipment

Slow Cooker, Cutting Board, Knife

Ingredients

- 500 g shrimp, peeled and deveined
- 300 g white fish fillets, cut into chunks
- 200 g smoked sausage, sliced
- 1 large bell pepper, chopped
- 1 medium onion, chopped
- 2 cloves garlic, minced
- 400 g canned tomatoes, diced
- 500 ml fish or chicken broth
- 2 tbsp olive oil
- 1 tbsp Cajun seasoning
- 1 tsp salt
- 1/2 tsp black pepper
- 1/2 tsp cayenne pepper (optional)
- 2 bay leaves

Directions

1. Heat olive oil in a pan over medium heat. Add the sausage slices and cook until browned.
2. In the slow cooker, combine the browned sausage, shrimp, fish, bell pepper, onion, garlic, tomatoes, and broth.
3. Stir in the Cajun seasoning, salt, black pepper, cayenne pepper, and bay leaves.
4. Cover and cook on low for 4 hours, or until the seafood is cooked through and flavors meld.
5. Remove bay leaves before serving. Adjust seasoning to taste if necessary.

Nutritional Information

Calories: 320, Protein: 35g, Carbohydrates: 8g, Fat: 18g, Fiber: 2g, Cholesterol: 180 mg, Salt: 950 mg, Potassium: 750 mg

HERB BUTTERED SCALLOPS

Delight in the rich, buttery flavor of scallops infused with aromatic herbs, all effortlessly cooked to perfection in your slow cooker. This low-carb dish is both elegant and simple, making it perfect for any occasion.

Equipment

Slow Cooker, Mixing Bowl, Measuring Spoons

Ingredients

- 500 g Scallops
- 100 g Unsalted Butter, softened
- 10 g Fresh Parsley, chopped
- 5 g Fresh Thyme, chopped
- 2 cloves Garlic, minced
- 5 ml Lemon Juice
- Salt and Pepper to taste

Directions

1. In a mixing bowl, combine the softened butter, parsley, thyme, garlic, lemon juice, salt, and pepper. Mix until well blended.
2. Place the scallops in the slow cooker and evenly spread the herb butter mixture over them.
3. Cover the slow cooker and cook on low for 2 hours, or until the scallops are tender and cooked through.
4. Occasionally stir gently to ensure even cooking and coating of the scallops with the herb butter.
5. Serve hot, garnished with additional fresh parsley if desired.

Nutritional Information

Calories: 320, Protein: 25g, Carbohydrates: 3g, Fat: 24g, Fiber: 0g, Cholesterol: 85 mg, Salt: 150 mg, Potassium: 450 mg

LEMON DILL WHITEFISH

Servings 4 | Prep: 10 min | Cook: 120 min

This Lemon Dill Whitefish is a delightful, low-carb dish that combines the freshness of lemon and dill with the delicate flavors of whitefish, all slowly cooked to perfection.

Equipment

Slow Cooker, Mixing Bowl, Measuring Cups

Ingredients

- 600 g Whitefish fillets
- 50 ml Fresh lemon juice
- 10 g Fresh dill, chopped
- 2 cloves Garlic, minced
- 30 ml Olive oil
- 5 g Salt
- 3 g Black pepper
- 100 g Cherry tomatoes, halved

Directions

1. In a mixing bowl, combine lemon juice, dill, garlic, olive oil, salt, and pepper.
2. Place the whitefish fillets in the slow cooker and pour the lemon-dill mixture over them.
3. Add cherry tomatoes around the fish.
4. Cover and cook on low for 2 hours, or until the fish flakes easily with a fork.
5. Serve warm, garnished with additional fresh dill if desired.

Nutritional Information

Calories: 220, Protein: 30g, Carbohydrates: 4g, Fat: 10g, Fiber: 1g, Cholesterol: 70 mg, Salt: 400 mg, Potassium: 600 mg

SLOW COOKER COCONUT SHRIMP SOUP

Servings 4 | Prep: 15 min | Cook: 240 min

Dive into a creamy, aromatic soup that combines the richness of coconut milk with tender shrimp, perfect for a low-carb diet.

Equipment

Slow Cooker, Knife, Cutting Board

Ingredients

- 500 g Shrimp, peeled and deveined
- 400 ml Coconut Milk
- 200 g Cauliflower, chopped
- 100 g Red Bell Pepper, sliced
- 50 g Onion, diced
- 2 cloves Garlic, minced
- 15 ml Fish Sauce
- 5 g Fresh Ginger, grated
- 5 g Red Curry Paste
- 10 g Fresh Cilantro, chopped

Directions

1. Place shrimp, cauliflower, red bell pepper, onion, and garlic in the slow cooker.
2. In a bowl, mix coconut milk, fish sauce, ginger, and red curry paste. Pour over the ingredients in the slow cooker.
3. Cover and cook on low for 4 hours.
4. Stir in fresh cilantro before serving.
5. Serve hot and enjoy the tropical flavors.

Nutritional Information

Calories: 320, Protein: 25g, Carbohydrates: 10g, Fat: 20g, Fiber: 3g, Cholesterol: 180 mg, Salt: 600 mg, Potassium: 450 mg

LOW CARB CIOPPINO

Servings 6 | Prep: 15 min | Cook: 240 min

A hearty and flavorful seafood stew, this low carb cioppino is perfect for a cozy meal. The slow cooker melds the flavors beautifully, making it a delightful dish for seafood lovers.

Equipment

Slow Cooker, Cutting Board, Knife

Ingredients

- 500g mixed seafood (shrimp, mussels, clams)
- 200g white fish fillets, cut into chunks
- 1 medium onion, chopped
- 3 cloves garlic, minced
- 400g canned tomatoes, crushed
- 500ml fish stock
- 100ml dry white wine
- 1 red bell pepper, chopped
- 1 tsp dried oregano
- 1 tsp dried basil
- Salt and pepper to taste
- 2 tbsp olive oil
- 1 tbsp fresh parsley, chopped (for garnish)

Directions

1. Heat olive oil in a pan over medium heat, sauté onion and garlic until translucent.
2. Transfer onion and garlic to the slow cooker. Add crushed tomatoes, fish stock, and white wine.
3. Stir in red bell pepper, oregano, basil, salt, and pepper.
4. Add mixed seafood and white fish chunks to the slow cooker.
5. Cover and cook on low for 4 hours until seafood is cooked through.
6. Garnish with fresh parsley before serving.

Nutritional Information

Calories: 220, Protein: 25g, Carbohydrates: 8g, Fat: 8g, Fiber: 2g, Cholesterol: 85mg, Salt: 600mg, Potassium: 750mg

CREAMY TUSCAN SALMON

Servings 4 | Prep: 10 min | Cook: 180 min

Indulge in the rich and savory flavors of Tuscan cuisine with this creamy salmon dish, perfectly crafted for a low-carb lifestyle. The slow cooker ensures the salmon remains tender and infused with the aromatic blend of herbs and spices.

Equipment

Slow Cooker, Mixing Bowl, Whisk

Ingredients

- 600 g Salmon Fillets
- 200 ml Heavy Cream
- 100 g Sun-Dried Tomatoes, chopped
- 100 g Fresh Spinach
- 50 g Parmesan Cheese, grated
- 2 cloves Garlic, minced
- 1 tbsp Olive Oil
- 1 tsp Dried Basil
- 1 tsp Dried Oregano
- Salt and Pepper to taste

Directions

1. Lightly grease the slow cooker with olive oil.
2. Place salmon fillets in the slow cooker and season with salt, pepper, basil, and oregano.
3. In a mixing bowl, whisk together heavy cream, minced garlic, and grated Parmesan cheese.
4. Pour the creamy mixture over the salmon fillets.
5. Add chopped sun-dried tomatoes and fresh spinach on top.
6. Cover and cook on low for 3 hours, or until the salmon is cooked through and tender.
7. Serve hot, garnished with additional Parmesan cheese if desired.

Nutritional Information

Calories: 450, Protein: 35g, Carbohydrates: 8g, Fat: 32g, Fiber: 2g, Cholesterol: 110 mg, Salt: 600 mg, Potassium: 900 mg

BEEF, PORK, AND LAMB RECIPES

SLOW COOKER BEEF STROGANOFF

Servings 6 | Prep: 15 min | Cook: 240 min

A comforting and creamy beef stroganoff made effortlessly in the slow cooker, perfect for a low-carb lifestyle. Tender beef and mushrooms in a rich, savory sauce make this dish a family favorite.

Equipment

Slow Cooker, Skillet, Mixing Bowl

Ingredients

- 1 kg beef chuck, cut into strips
- 200 g mushrooms, sliced
- 1 onion, chopped
- 3 cloves garlic, minced
- 250 ml beef broth
- 200 ml sour cream
- 2 tbsp Dijon mustard
- 1 tbsp olive oil
- Salt and pepper to taste
- 1 tbsp fresh parsley, chopped (for garnish)

Directions

1. Heat olive oil in a skillet over medium heat. Add beef strips and brown on all sides.
2. Transfer the beef to the slow cooker. Add mushrooms, onion, and garlic.
3. In a mixing bowl, combine beef broth, sour cream, and Dijon mustard. Pour over the beef and vegetables in the slow cooker.
4. Season with salt and pepper. Cover and cook on low for 4 hours or until the beef is tender.
5. Stir well before serving. Garnish with fresh parsley.

Nutritional Information

Calories: 350, Protein: 30g, Carbohydrates: 6g, Fat: 22g, Fiber: 1g, Cholesterol: 95 mg, Salt: 450 mg, Potassium: 650 mg

KETO-FRIENDLY PULLED PORK

Servings 6 | Prep: 15 min | Cook: 480 min

This succulent, keto-friendly pulled pork is slow-cooked to perfection, offering a tender and flavorful dish that's low in carbs and high in satisfaction.

Equipment

Slow Cooker, Mixing Bowl, Fork

Ingredients

- 1.5 kg Pork Shoulder
- 200 ml Sugar-Free BBQ Sauce
- 30 ml Apple Cider Vinegar
- 15 g Smoked Paprika
- 10 g Garlic Powder
- 10 g Onion Powder
- 5 g Salt
- 5 g Black Pepper

Directions

1. Rub the pork shoulder with smoked paprika, garlic powder, onion powder, salt, and black pepper.
2. Place the seasoned pork shoulder into the slow cooker.
3. Pour the apple cider vinegar and sugar-free BBQ sauce over the pork.
4. Cover and cook on low for 8 hours, or until the pork is tender and easily shredded.
5. Once cooked, remove the pork from the slow cooker and shred it using a fork.
6. Return the shredded pork to the slow cooker and mix it with the juices.
7. Serve warm, garnished with additional BBQ sauce if desired.

Nutritional Information

Calories: 320, Protein: 28g, Carbohydrates: 4g, Fat: 22g, Fiber: 1g, Cholesterol: 95 mg, Salt: 600 mg, Potassium: 450 mg

GARLIC BUTTER LAMB CHOPS

Servings 4 | Prep: 15 min | Cook: 240 min

Succulent lamb chops infused with rich garlic butter, slow-cooked to perfection for a tender, flavorful dish that melts in your mouth.

Equipment

Slow Cooker, Skillet, Mixing Bowl

Ingredients

- 800 g lamb chops
- 50 g unsalted butter
- 5 cloves garlic, minced
- 10 g fresh rosemary, chopped
- 5 g salt
- 3 g black pepper
- 100 ml chicken broth
- 30 ml lemon juice

Directions

1. Season the lamb chops with salt and pepper on both sides.
2. In a skillet, melt the butter over medium heat. Add minced garlic and rosemary, sautéing until fragrant.
3. Sear the lamb chops in the skillet for 2-3 minutes on each side until browned.
4. Transfer the lamb chops to the slow cooker. Pour in chicken broth and lemon juice.
5. Drizzle the garlic butter mixture over the lamb chops.
6. Cover and cook on low for 4 hours, or until the lamb is tender.
7. Serve hot, garnished with additional rosemary if desired.

Nutritional Information

Calories: 450, Protein: 35g, Carbohydrates: 2g, Fat: 34g, Fiber: 0g, Cholesterol: 120 mg, Salt: 600 mg, Potassium: 450 mg

SLOW COOKER BEEF BRISKET

Servings 6 | Prep: 15 min | Cook: 480 min

This slow cooker beef brisket is tender, juicy, and infused with rich flavors, perfect for a comforting low-carb meal.

Equipment

Slow Cooker, Mixing Bowl, Knife

Ingredients

- 1.5 kg Beef Brisket
- 30 ml Olive Oil
- 200 g Onion, sliced
- 4 cloves Garlic, minced
- 250 ml Beef Broth
- 60 ml Soy Sauce
- 30 ml Apple Cider Vinegar
- 5 g Smoked Paprika
- 5 g Black Pepper
- 5 g Salt

Directions

1. Rub the beef brisket with olive oil, smoked paprika, black pepper, and salt.
2. Place the sliced onions and minced garlic at the bottom of the slow cooker.
3. Lay the seasoned brisket on top of the onions and garlic.
4. In a mixing bowl, combine beef broth, soy sauce, and apple cider vinegar. Pour over the brisket.
5. Cover and cook on low for 8 hours, or until the brisket is tender and easily shredded.
6. Once cooked, remove the brisket and let it rest for 10 minutes before slicing.
7. Serve with the juices from the slow cooker for added flavor.

Nutritional Information

Calories: 450, Protein: 40g, Carbohydrates: 5g, Fat: 30g, Fiber: 1g, Cholesterol: 120 mg, Salt: 800 mg, Potassium: 700 mg

LOW CARB KOREAN SHORT RIBS

Servings 4 | Prep: 15 min | Cook: 480 min

These tender, flavorful Korean short ribs are a low-carb delight, slow-cooked to perfection with a savory blend of spices and sauces.

Equipment

Slow Cooker, Mixing Bowl, Measuring Cups and Spoons

Ingredients

- 1 kg Beef Short Ribs
- 60 ml Soy Sauce (low sodium)
- 30 ml Sesame Oil
- 30 g Fresh Ginger, grated
- 4 cloves Garlic, minced
- 15 g Erythritol or preferred low-carb sweetener
- 5 g Red Pepper Flakes
- 60 ml Rice Vinegar
- 2 Green Onions, chopped
- 15 g Sesame Seeds

Directions

1. In a mixing bowl, combine soy sauce, sesame oil, ginger, garlic, erythritol, red pepper flakes, and rice vinegar. Mix well.
2. Place the beef short ribs in the slow cooker. Pour the sauce mixture over the ribs, ensuring they are well coated.
3. Cover and cook on low for 8 hours, or until the ribs are tender and the meat easily falls off the bone.
4. Once cooked, remove the ribs from the slow cooker and garnish with chopped green onions and sesame seeds.
5. Serve hot and enjoy your low-carb Korean short ribs.

Nutritional Information

Calories: 450, Protein: 30g, Carbohydrates: 5g, Fat: 35g, Fiber: 1g, Cholesterol: 100 mg, Salt: 800 mg, Potassium: 450 mg

HERB-CRUSTED PORK TENDERLOIN

Servings 4 | Prep: 15 min | Cook: 240 min

This herb-crusted pork tenderloin is a succulent and flavorful dish, perfect for a low-carb diet. The slow cooker ensures the pork remains tender and juicy, while the herb crust adds a delightful aromatic touch.

Equipment

Slow Cooker, Mixing Bowl, Measuring Spoons

Ingredients

- 800 g Pork Tenderloin
- 30 ml Olive Oil
- 10 g Fresh Rosemary, chopped
- 10 g Fresh Thyme, chopped
- 5 g Garlic Powder
- 5 g Onion Powder
- 5 g Salt
- 2 g Black Pepper

Directions

1. In a mixing bowl, combine olive oil, rosemary, thyme, garlic powder, onion powder, salt, and black pepper to create a herb mixture.
2. Rub the herb mixture evenly over the pork tenderloin, ensuring it is well-coated.
3. Place the pork tenderloin in the slow cooker.
4. Cover and cook on low for 4 hours, or until the pork reaches an internal temperature of 63°C.
5. Once cooked, remove the pork from the slow cooker and let it rest for 5 minutes before slicing and serving.

Nutritional Information

Calories: 320, Protein: 35g, Carbohydrates: 2g, Fat: 20g, Fiber: 1g, Cholesterol: 95 mg, Salt: 600 mg, Potassium: 750 mg

SLOW COOKER ITALIAN MEATBALLS

Servings 6 | Prep: 15 min | Cook: 240 min

These tender and flavorful Italian meatballs are perfect for a low-carb diet, simmered slowly to perfection in a rich tomato sauce.

Equipment

Slow Cooker, Mixing Bowl, Skillet

Ingredients

- 500 g Ground Beef
- 100 g Ground Pork
- 50 g Parmesan Cheese, grated
- 1 Egg
- 100 g Almond Flour
- 2 cloves Garlic, minced
- 5 g Dried Oregano
- 5 g Dried Basil
- 500 ml Tomato Sauce
- 10 ml Olive Oil
- Salt and Pepper to taste

Directions

1. In a mixing bowl, combine ground beef, ground pork, Parmesan cheese, egg, almond flour, garlic, oregano, basil, salt, and pepper. Mix until well combined.
2. Form the mixture into small meatballs, about 3 cm in diameter.
3. Heat olive oil in a skillet over medium heat. Brown the meatballs on all sides, then transfer them to the slow cooker.
4. Pour the tomato sauce over the meatballs in the slow cooker.
5. Cover and cook on low for 4 hours, until the meatballs are cooked through and tender.
6. Serve hot, garnished with additional Parmesan cheese if desired.

Nutritional Information

Calories: 320, Protein: 25g, Carbohydrates: 8g, Fat: 22g, Fiber: 3g, Cholesterol: 85 mg, Salt: 450 mg, Potassium: 600 mg

CREAMY MUSTARD PORK CHOPS

Servings 4 | Prep: 10 min | Cook: 240 min

Indulge in tender pork chops enveloped in a rich, creamy mustard sauce, perfect for a low-carb lifestyle.

Equipment

Slow Cooker, Mixing Bowl, Whisk

Ingredients

- 800 g Pork Chops
- 200 ml Heavy Cream
- 60 ml Dijon Mustard
- 1 Onion, finely chopped
- 2 Garlic Cloves, minced
- 15 ml Olive Oil
- 5 g Fresh Thyme
- Salt and Pepper to taste

Directions

1. Heat olive oil in a pan over medium heat and sear pork chops until browned on both sides.
2. Transfer pork chops to the slow cooker.
3. In a mixing bowl, whisk together heavy cream, Dijon mustard, onion, garlic, thyme, salt, and pepper.
4. Pour the creamy mustard mixture over the pork chops in the slow cooker.
5. Cover and cook on low for 4 hours or until the pork is tender.
6. Serve the pork chops with the creamy sauce drizzled on top.

Nutritional Information

Calories: 450, Protein: 35g, Carbohydrates: 5g, Fat: 32g, Fiber: 1g, Cholesterol: 120 mg, Salt: 450 mg, Potassium: 600 mg

ROSEMARY GARLIC LAMB SHANK

Servings 4 | Prep: 15 min | Cook: 480 min

Savor the tender, aromatic flavors of lamb shank infused with rosemary and garlic, slow-cooked to perfection for a hearty, low-carb delight.

Equipment

Slow Cooker, Skillet, Tongs

Ingredients

- 1.5 kg Lamb Shanks
- 30 ml Olive Oil
- 4 cloves Garlic, minced
- 10 g Fresh Rosemary, chopped
- 200 ml Beef Broth
- 100 ml Red Wine
- 5 g Salt
- 3 g Black Pepper
- 1 Onion, sliced

Directions

1. Heat olive oil in a skillet over medium heat. Sear lamb shanks until browned on all sides.
2. Transfer lamb shanks to the slow cooker.
3. In the same skillet, sauté garlic and onion until fragrant. Add rosemary, salt, and pepper.
4. Pour in beef broth and red wine, stirring to combine. Bring to a simmer.
5. Pour the mixture over the lamb shanks in the slow cooker.
6. Cover and cook on low for 8 hours, until the lamb is tender and falling off the bone.
7. Serve hot, garnished with additional rosemary if desired.

Nutritional Information

Calories: 520, Protein: 45g, Carbohydrates: 4g, Fat: 35g, Fiber: 1g, Cholesterol: 140 mg, Salt: 600 mg, Potassium: 750 mg

KETO BARBECUE PORK RIBS

Servings 4 | Prep: 15 min | Cook: 480 min

Succulent and tender, these Keto Barbecue Pork Ribs are slow-cooked to perfection, offering a smoky flavor with a hint of sweetness, all while keeping it low-carb. Perfect for a hearty meal without the guilt.

Equipment

Slow Cooker, Mixing Bowl, Basting Brush

Ingredients

- 1.5 kg Pork Ribs
- 200 ml Sugar-Free Barbecue Sauce
- 30 g Smoked Paprika
- 15 g Garlic Powder
- 15 g Onion Powder
- 10 g Salt
- 5 g Black Pepper
- 5 g Chili Powder
- 30 ml Apple Cider Vinegar

Directions

1. In a mixing bowl, combine smoked paprika, garlic powder, onion powder, salt, black pepper, and chili powder.
2. Rub the spice mixture evenly over the pork ribs.
3. Place the ribs in the slow cooker and pour apple cider vinegar over them.
4. Cover and cook on low for 8 hours, or until the ribs are tender.
5. In the last 30 minutes of cooking, brush the ribs with sugar-free barbecue sauce.
6. Optional: For a caramelized finish, transfer ribs to a baking sheet and broil in the oven for 5 minutes.

Nutritional Information

Calories: 480, Protein: 40g, Carbohydrates: 5g, Fat: 35g, Fiber: 1g, Cholesterol: 120 mg, Salt: 600 mg, Potassium: 750 mg

SPICY BEEF CHILI (NO BEANS)

This hearty and spicy beef chili is perfect for those chilly days. Packed with flavor and free of beans, it's a low-carb delight that simmers to perfection in your slow cooker.

Equipment

Slow Cooker, Skillet, Wooden Spoon

Ingredients

- 1 kg ground beef
- 200 g bell peppers, diced
- 150 g onions, diced
- 4 cloves garlic, minced
- 400 g canned tomatoes, crushed
- 50 g tomato paste
- 30 ml olive oil
- 15 g chili powder
- 10 g cumin powder
- 5 g smoked paprika
- 5 g salt
- 2 g black pepper
- 1 g cayenne pepper (optional, for extra heat)

Directions

1. Heat olive oil in a skillet over medium heat. Add onions and garlic, sauté until translucent.
2. Add ground beef to the skillet, cook until browned. Drain excess fat.
3. Transfer beef mixture to the slow cooker. Add bell peppers, crushed tomatoes, and tomato paste.
4. Stir in chili powder, cumin, smoked paprika, salt, black pepper, and cayenne pepper.
5. Cover and cook on low for 6 hours, stirring occasionally.
6. Adjust seasoning to taste before serving.

Nutritional Information

Calories: 350, Protein: 28g, Carbohydrates: 10g, Fat: 22g, Fiber: 3g, Cholesterol: 80 mg, Salt: 600 mg, Potassium: 750 mg

LOW CARB BEEF BOURGUIGNON

A classic French dish made low-carb, this Beef Bourguignon is rich in flavor with tender beef, aromatic vegetables, and a savory broth, all slow-cooked to perfection.

Equipment

Slow Cooker, Skillet, Cutting Board

Ingredients

- 1 kg beef chuck, cut into 4 cm cubes
- 200 g bacon, diced
- 250 g mushrooms, sliced
- 150 g carrots, sliced
- 1 onion, chopped
- 3 cloves garlic, minced
- 500 ml dry red wine
- 250 ml beef broth
- 2 tbsp tomato paste
- 1 tsp thyme
- 2 bay leaves
- Salt and pepper to taste
- 2 tbsp olive oil

Directions

1. Heat olive oil in a skillet over medium heat. Add bacon and cook until crispy. Remove and set aside.
2. In the same skillet, sear the beef cubes until browned on all sides. Transfer to the slow cooker.
3. Add mushrooms, carrots, onion, and garlic to the skillet. Sauté for 5 minutes, then add to the slow cooker.
4. Pour red wine and beef broth into the slow cooker. Stir in tomato paste, thyme, bay leaves, salt, and pepper.
5. Cover and cook on low for 8 hours, or until the beef is tender. Remove bay leaves before serving.

Nutritional Information

Calories: 450, Protein: 40g, Carbohydrates: 8g, Fat: 25g, Fiber: 2g, Cholesterol: 110 mg, Salt: 800 mg, Potassium: 900 mg

SLOW COOKER PORK CARNITAS

Servings 6 | Prep: 15 min | Cook: 480 min

These slow cooker pork carnitas are tender, flavorful, and perfect for a low-carb meal. The slow cooking process infuses the pork with spices, resulting in juicy and delicious carnitas that can be served in lettuce wraps or over a salad.

Equipment

Slow Cooker, Skillet, Fork

Ingredients

- 1.5 kg pork shoulder, boneless
- 15 ml olive oil
- 10 g garlic, minced
- 5 g ground cumin
- 5 g smoked paprika
- 5 g dried oregano
- 5 g salt
- 2 g black pepper
- 250 ml chicken broth
- 60 ml lime juice
- 1 onion, sliced
- 1 jalapeño, sliced (optional)

Directions

1. Rub the pork shoulder with olive oil, garlic, cumin, smoked paprika, oregano, salt, and pepper.
2. Place the seasoned pork in the slow cooker and add chicken broth, lime juice, onion, and jalapeño.
3. Cover and cook on low for 8 hours, or until the pork is tender and easily shredded with a fork.
4. Remove the pork from the slow cooker and shred it using two forks.
5. Heat a skillet over medium-high heat and add the shredded pork to crisp the edges slightly.
6. Serve the pork carnitas in lettuce wraps or over a salad for a low-carb meal.

Nutritional Information

Calories: 350, Protein: 45g, Carbohydrates: 3g, Fat: 18g, Fiber: 1g, Cholesterol: 120 mg, Salt: 600 mg, Potassium: 750 mg

GREEK-STYLE LAMB STEW

Servings 6 | Prep: 15 min | Cook: 480 min

This Greek-style lamb stew is a hearty and flavorful dish, perfect for a low-carb diet. The slow cooking process ensures tender meat infused with Mediterranean spices.

Equipment

Slow Cooker, Cutting Board, Knife

Ingredients

- 1 kg lamb shoulder, cubed
- 30 ml olive oil
- 200 g onion, chopped
- 3 cloves garlic, minced
- 400 g canned tomatoes, chopped
- 100 g Kalamata olives, pitted and halved
- 1 lemon, juiced
- 5 g dried oregano
- 5 g ground cinnamon
- Salt and pepper to taste
- 200 ml beef broth
- 50 g feta cheese, crumbled (optional garnish)
- Fresh parsley, chopped (optional garnish)

Directions

1. Heat olive oil in a pan over medium heat. Brown the lamb cubes on all sides.
2. Transfer the browned lamb to the slow cooker.
3. In the same pan, sauté onions and garlic until softened, then add to the slow cooker.
4. Add canned tomatoes, olives, lemon juice, oregano, cinnamon, salt, and pepper to the slow cooker.
5. Pour in the beef broth and stir to combine all ingredients.
6. Cover and cook on low for 8 hours, or until the lamb is tender.
7. Serve hot, garnished with crumbled feta and fresh parsley if desired.

Nutritional Information

Calories: 450, Protein: 35g, Carbohydrates: 10g, Fat: 30g, Fiber: 3g, Cholesterol: 110 mg, Salt: 700 mg, Potassium: 600 mg

BEEF AND MUSHROOM CASEROLE

Servings 4 | Prep: 15 min | Cook: 240 min

A hearty and savory casserole that combines tender beef with earthy mushrooms, perfect for a comforting low-carb meal.

Equipment

Slow Cooker, Skillet, Mixing Bowl

Ingredients

- 500g Beef Stew Meat
- 200g Mushrooms, sliced
- 1 Onion, chopped
- 2 Cloves Garlic, minced
- 200ml Beef Broth
- 100ml Heavy Cream
- 1 tbsp Olive Oil
- 1 tsp Dried Thyme
- Salt and Pepper to taste

Directions

1. Heat olive oil in a skillet over medium heat. Add beef stew meat and brown on all sides.
2. Transfer the browned beef to the slow cooker.
3. In the same skillet, add onions and garlic, sauté until onions are translucent.
4. Add mushrooms to the skillet and cook until they release their moisture.
5. Transfer the onion, garlic, and mushroom mixture to the slow cooker.
6. Pour beef broth and heavy cream over the ingredients in the slow cooker. Add thyme, salt, and pepper.
7. Cover and cook on low for 4 hours or until the beef is tender.

Nutritional Information

Calories: 350, Protein: 30g, Carbohydrates: 8g, Fat: 22g, Fiber: 2g, Cholesterol: 90mg, Salt: 600mg, Potassium: 700mg

SLOW COOKER TACO BEEF

Servings 6 | Prep: 15 min | Cook: 360 min

This Slow Cooker Taco Beef is a flavorful, low-carb dish perfect for taco nights. The slow cooking process infuses the beef with spices, creating a tender and delicious filling for your favorite low-carb tortillas or lettuce wraps.

Equipment

Slow Cooker, Skillet, Mixing Bowl

Ingredients

- 1 kg beef chuck roast, cut into chunks
- 15 ml olive oil
- 200 g onion, chopped
- 3 cloves garlic, minced
- 15 g chili powder
- 5 g ground cumin
- 5 g smoked paprika
- 5 g salt
- 2 g black pepper
- 100 ml beef broth
- 30 ml lime juice
- 10 g fresh cilantro, chopped

Directions

1. Heat olive oil in a skillet over medium heat. Brown the beef chunks on all sides.
2. Transfer the beef to the slow cooker. Add onion, garlic, chili powder, cumin, smoked paprika, salt, and pepper.
3. Pour beef broth over the mixture. Cover and cook on low for 6 hours, or until beef is tender.
4. Once cooked, shred the beef using two forks. Stir in lime juice and fresh cilantro.
5. Serve in low-carb tortillas or lettuce wraps, garnished with your favorite toppings.

Nutritional Information

Calories: 320, Protein: 35g, Carbohydrates: 4g, Fat: 18g, Fiber: 1g, Cholesterol: 95 mg, Salt: 480 mg, Potassium: 650 mg

KETO MEATLOAF IN SLOW COOKER

Servings 6 | Prep: 15 min | Cook: 240 min

This keto meatloaf is a savory delight, perfectly cooked in a slow cooker to maintain its juiciness and rich flavors. It's a comforting, low-carb meal that satisfies without the guilt.

Equipment

Slow Cooker, Mixing Bowl, Measuring Cups and Spoons

Ingredients

- 500 g Ground Beef
- 250 g Ground Pork
- 100 g Almond Flour
- 2 Eggs
- 100 ml Unsweetened Tomato Sauce
- 50 g Onion, finely chopped
- 3 cloves Garlic, minced
- 10 g Italian Seasoning
- 5 g Salt
- 5 g Black Pepper
- 30 ml Worcestershire Sauce

Directions

1. In a mixing bowl, combine ground beef, ground pork, almond flour, eggs, onion, garlic, Italian seasoning, salt, and pepper. Mix until well combined.
2. Shape the mixture into a loaf and place it in the slow cooker.
3. In a small bowl, mix the tomato sauce and Worcestershire sauce. Pour over the meatloaf.
4. Cover and cook on low for 4 hours or until the internal temperature reaches 70°C.
5. Let the meatloaf rest for 10 minutes before slicing and serving.

Nutritional Information

Calories: 350, Protein: 25g, Carbohydrates: 5g, Fat: 25g, Fiber: 2g, Cholesterol: 120 mg, Salt: 600 mg, Potassium: 450 mg

GARLIC & HERB CRUSTED ROAST BEEF

Servings 6 | Prep: 15 min | Cook: 480 min

This succulent roast beef is infused with a flavorful garlic and herb crust, making it a perfect centerpiece for any low-carb meal. The slow cooker ensures the meat is tender and juicy, while the aromatic herbs create a delightful crust.

Equipment

Slow Cooker, Mixing Bowl, Knife

Ingredients

- 1.5 kg Beef Roast
- 30 g Fresh Garlic, minced
- 15 g Fresh Rosemary, chopped
- 15 g Fresh Thyme, chopped
- 10 g Salt
- 5 g Black Pepper
- 30 ml Olive Oil

Directions

1. In a mixing bowl, combine minced garlic, rosemary, thyme, salt, pepper, and olive oil to form a paste.
2. Rub the garlic and herb paste evenly over the beef roast, ensuring it is well-coated.
3. Place the beef roast in the slow cooker.
4. Cover and cook on low for 8 hours, or until the beef is tender and cooked to your desired doneness.
5. Once cooked, remove the roast from the slow cooker and let it rest for 10 minutes before slicing.

Nutritional Information

Calories: 350, Protein: 45g, Carbohydrates: 2g, Fat: 18g, Fiber: 0g, Cholesterol: 120 mg, Salt: 400 mg, Potassium: 750 mg

SLOW COOKER PEPPER STEAK

Servings 4 | Prep: 15 min | Cook: 240 min

This slow cooker pepper steak is a savory and satisfying low-carb dish, featuring tender beef strips and vibrant bell peppers in a rich, flavorful sauce. Perfect for a comforting meal without the carbs.

Equipment

Slow Cooker, Cutting Board, Knife

Ingredients

- 500 g beef sirloin, thinly sliced
- 2 bell peppers (one red, one green), sliced
- 1 onion, sliced
- 3 cloves garlic, minced
- 60 ml soy sauce
- 30 ml beef broth
- 15 ml olive oil
- 5 g ground black pepper
- 5 g salt

Directions

1. Heat olive oil in a pan over medium heat and brown the beef slices.
2. Transfer the beef to the slow cooker.
3. Add sliced bell peppers, onion, and minced garlic to the slow cooker.
4. Pour soy sauce and beef broth over the ingredients.
5. Season with ground black pepper and salt.
6. Cover and cook on low for 4 hours, or until the beef is tender.
7. Stir well before serving.

Nutritional Information

Calories: 320, Protein: 35g, Carbohydrates: 8g, Fat: 18g, Fiber: 2g, Cholesterol: 80 mg, Salt: 900 mg, Potassium: 650 mg

ASIAN-INSPIRED PORK BELLY

Servings 4 | Prep: 15 min | Cook: 240 min

This Asian-inspired pork belly is a succulent and flavorful dish that combines the richness of pork with aromatic spices, creating a melt-in-your-mouth experience. Perfect for a low-carb meal, it's both satisfying and easy to prepare in a slow cooker.

Equipment

Slow Cooker, Mixing Bowl, Measuring Cups and Spoons

Ingredients

- 800 g pork belly, skin scored
- 60 ml soy sauce
- 30 ml rice vinegar
- 15 g fresh ginger, grated
- 4 cloves garlic, minced
- 5 g five-spice powder
- 10 ml sesame oil
- 2 g chili flakes (optional)
- 100 ml water
- 2 green onions, sliced for garnish

Directions

1. In a mixing bowl, combine soy sauce, rice vinegar, ginger, garlic, five-spice powder, sesame oil, and chili flakes. Mix well.
2. Place the pork belly in the slow cooker and pour the sauce mixture over it, ensuring the pork is well-coated.
3. Add water to the slow cooker, cover, and cook on low for 4 hours or until the pork is tender.
4. Once cooked, remove the pork belly and let it rest for a few minutes before slicing.
5. Garnish with sliced green onions and serve.

Nutritional Information

Calories: 520, Protein: 25g, Carbohydrates: 3g, Fat: 45g, Fiber: 0g, Cholesterol: 80 mg, Salt: 900 mg, Potassium: 350 mg

SAUCES AND CONDIMENTS

SLOW COOKER SUGAR-FREE BBQ SAUCE

Servings 10 | Prep: 10 min | Cook: 120 min

This tangy and smoky sugar-free BBQ sauce is perfect for those looking to enjoy classic barbecue flavors without the carbs. Made effortlessly in a slow cooker, it's a versatile condiment for meats, sandwiches, and more.

Equipment

Slow Cooker, Whisk, Measuring Cups and Spoons

Ingredients

- 500 ml Tomato Puree
- 100 ml Apple Cider Vinegar
- 50 g Erythritol
- 30 g Smoked Paprika
- 20 g Garlic Powder
- 20 g Onion Powder
- 10 g Mustard Powder
- 5 g Black Pepper
- 5 g Salt
- 5 ml Liquid Smoke
- 2 g Cayenne Pepper (optional for heat)

Directions

1. Combine all ingredients in the slow cooker and whisk until smooth.
2. Cover and cook on low for 2 hours, stirring occasionally.
3. Taste and adjust seasoning if necessary.
4. Allow the sauce to cool slightly before transferring to a jar or bottle.
5. Store in the refrigerator for up to 2 weeks.

Nutritional Information

Calories: 20, Protein: 1g, Carbohydrates: 4g, Fat: 0g, Fiber: 1g, Cholesterol: 0 mg, Salt: 200 mg, Potassium: 150 mg

KETO ALFREDO SAUCE

Servings 8 | Prep: 10 min | Cook: 60 min

This rich and creamy Keto Alfredo Sauce is perfect for those following a low-carb lifestyle. Made in a slow cooker, it's an effortless way to enjoy a classic sauce with a keto twist.

Equipment

Slow Cooker, Whisk, Measuring Cups and Spoons

Ingredients

- 500 ml Heavy Cream
- 150 g Cream Cheese, cubed
- 100 g Parmesan Cheese, grated
- 50 g Unsalted Butter
- 5 g Garlic, minced
- 2 g Black Pepper
- 2 g Salt
- 5 g Fresh Parsley, chopped (optional)

Directions

1. Add the heavy cream, cream cheese, Parmesan cheese, and butter to the slow cooker.
2. Stir in the minced garlic, black pepper, and salt.
3. Cover and cook on low for 60 minutes, stirring occasionally until the cheese is melted and the sauce is smooth.
4. Once done, whisk the sauce to ensure it is well combined.
5. Serve warm, garnished with fresh parsley if desired.

Nutritional Information

Calories: 320, Protein: 6g, Carbohydrates: 3g, Fat: 32g, Fiber: 0g, Cholesterol: 90 mg, Salt: 300 mg, Potassium: 100 mg

CREAMY AVOCADO DRESSING

Servings 4 | Prep: 10 min | Cook: 0 min

This creamy avocado dressing is a luscious, low-carb addition to salads or as a dip, offering a rich, tangy flavor with a smooth texture.

Equipment

Blender, Measuring Cups, Measuring Spoons

Ingredients

- 200 g ripe avocado (about 1 large avocado)
- 60 ml olive oil
- 30 ml lime juice (freshly squeezed)
- 50 g Greek yogurt
- 10 g fresh cilantro leaves
- 1 clove garlic, minced
- 2 g salt
- 1 g black pepper
- 30 ml water (adjust for desired consistency)

Directions

1. Cut the avocado in half, remove the pit, and scoop the flesh into a blender.
2. Add olive oil, lime juice, Greek yogurt, cilantro, minced garlic, salt, and black pepper to the blender.
3. Blend on high speed until the mixture is smooth and creamy.
4. Gradually add water to the blender, blending until you reach your desired consistency.
5. Taste and adjust seasoning if necessary.

Nutritional Information

Calories: 180, Protein: 2g, Carbohydrates: 5g, Fat: 18g, Fiber: 3g, Cholesterol: 2mg, Salt: 150mg, Potassium: 350mg

LOW CARB SPICY BUFFALO SAUCE

Servings 10 | Prep: 5 min | Cook: 30 min

A fiery and tangy sauce perfect for wings, veggies, or as a zesty condiment. This low-carb version retains all the flavor without the extra carbs.

Equipment

Slow Cooker, Whisk, Measuring Cups

Ingredients

- 240 ml Hot Sauce
- 100 g Unsalted Butter
- 15 ml Apple Cider Vinegar
- 5 g Garlic Powder
- 5 g Onion Powder
- 2 g Paprika
- 1 g Cayenne Pepper (adjust for desired heat)
- 2 g Salt

Directions

1. Add hot sauce, butter, apple cider vinegar, garlic powder, onion powder, paprika, cayenne pepper, and salt into the slow cooker.
2. Set the slow cooker to low heat and cover.
3. Cook for 30 minutes, stirring occasionally to ensure the butter melts and ingredients combine well.
4. Once cooked, whisk the sauce until smooth and well-blended.
5. Allow to cool slightly before serving or storing in an airtight container.

Nutritional Information

Calories: 50, Protein: 0.5g, Carbohydrates: 0.5g, Fat: 5g, Fiber: 0g, Cholesterol: 15 mg, Salt: 200 mg, Potassium: 20 mg

SLOW COOKER TOMATO BASIL MARINARA

Servings 8 | Prep: 10 min | Cook: 240 min

This rich and flavorful tomato basil marinara is perfect for pasta, zoodles, or as a base for your favorite Italian dishes. Made effortlessly in a slow cooker, it's a low-carb delight that brings out the natural sweetness of tomatoes and the aromatic essence of basil.

Equipment

Slow Cooker, Cutting Board, Knife

Ingredients

- 1 kg ripe tomatoes, chopped
- 100 g onion, finely chopped
- 4 cloves garlic, minced
- 60 ml olive oil
- 15 g fresh basil leaves, chopped
- 5 g dried oregano
- 5 g salt
- 2 g black pepper
- 30 ml balsamic vinegar

Directions

1. Add the chopped tomatoes, onion, and garlic to the slow cooker.
2. Drizzle olive oil over the mixture and stir in the basil, oregano, salt, and pepper.
3. Cover and cook on low for 4 hours, stirring occasionally.
4. Once cooked, use an immersion blender to achieve desired sauce consistency.
5. Stir in balsamic vinegar and adjust seasoning if necessary.
6. Serve warm or store in airtight containers for later use.

Nutritional Information

Calories: 85, Protein: 2g, Carbohydrates: 10g, Fat: 5g, Fiber: 3g, Cholesterol: 0 mg, Salt: 300 mg, Potassium: 400 mg

KETO HONEY MUSTARD DRESSING

Servings 8 | Prep: 10 min | Cook: 0 min

This Keto Honey Mustard Dressing is a perfect blend of tangy and sweet flavors, without the carbs. Ideal for salads or as a dipping sauce, it brings a delightful twist to your meals.

Equipment

Blender, Measuring Cups, Measuring Spoons

Ingredients

- 120 ml Olive Oil
- 60 ml Apple Cider Vinegar
- 50 g Dijon Mustard
- 30 g Sugar-Free Honey Substitute
- 5 g Garlic Powder
- 5 g Onion Powder
- 2 g Salt
- 1 g Black Pepper

Directions

1. Combine all ingredients in a blender.
2. Blend on high speed until smooth and emulsified.
3. Taste and adjust seasoning if necessary.
4. Transfer to a jar or bottle for storage.
5. Refrigerate for at least 30 minutes before serving to allow flavors to meld.

Nutritional Information

Calories: 150, Protein: 0g, Carbohydrates: 1g, Fat: 16g, Fiber: 0g, Cholesterol: 0mg, Salt: 250mg, Potassium: 10mg

SUGAR-FREE SWEET AND SOUR SAUCE

Servings 8 | Prep: 10 min | Cook: 120 min

This sugar-free sweet and sour sauce is a perfect balance of tangy and sweet, ideal for enhancing your favorite dishes without the extra carbs.

Equipment

Slow Cooker, Whisk, Measuring Cups

Ingredients

- 240 ml Apple Cider Vinegar
- 120 ml Soy Sauce (low sodium)
- 100 g Erythritol
- 60 ml Tomato Paste
- 1 tsp Garlic Powder
- 1 tsp Onion Powder
- 1 tsp Ground Ginger
- 1/2 tsp Xanthan Gum

Directions

1. Combine apple cider vinegar, soy sauce, erythritol, and tomato paste in the slow cooker.
2. Add garlic powder, onion powder, and ground ginger, whisking until well mixed.
3. Cover and cook on low for 2 hours, stirring occasionally.
4. In the last 15 minutes, whisk in the xanthan gum to thicken the sauce.
5. Allow the sauce to cool slightly before serving or storing.

Nutritional Information

Calories: 15, Protein: 0.5g, Carbohydrates: 3g, Fat: 0g, Fiber: 0g, Cholesterol: 0 mg, Salt: 300 mg, Potassium: 50 mg

SLOW COOKER ROASTED GARLIC BUTTER

Servings 8 | Prep: 10 min | Cook: 240 min

This rich and aromatic roasted garlic butter is perfect for enhancing the flavor of meats, vegetables, or as a spread. The slow cooker method ensures a deep, mellow garlic flavor without the need for constant attention.

Equipment

Slow Cooker, Mixing Bowl, Whisk

Ingredients

- 200 g Unsalted Butter, softened
- 100 g Garlic Cloves, peeled
- 15 ml Olive Oil
- 5 g Fresh Thyme Leaves
- 2 g Salt
- 1 g Black Pepper

Directions

1. Place the garlic cloves in the slow cooker and drizzle with olive oil.
2. Cook on low for 4 hours until the garlic is soft and caramelized.
3. In a mixing bowl, combine the softened butter, roasted garlic, thyme, salt, and pepper.
4. Use a whisk to blend until smooth and well combined.
5. Transfer the garlic butter to a container and refrigerate until firm.

Nutritional Information

Calories: 150, Protein: 0.5g, Carbohydrates: 1g, Fat: 16g, Fiber: 0g, Cholesterol: 40 mg, Salt: 100 mg, Potassium: 20 mg

LOW CARB CILANTRO LIME DRESSING

Servings 8 | Prep: 10 min | Cook: 0 min

This vibrant and zesty cilantro lime dressing is perfect for adding a fresh, tangy kick to your salads or grilled meats. Made in a slow cooker, it infuses flavors beautifully while keeping it low in carbs.

Equipment

Blender, Slow Cooker, Measuring Cups

Ingredients

- 100 ml Olive Oil
- 50 ml Lime Juice
- 30 g Fresh Cilantro Leaves
- 2 cloves Garlic, minced
- 5 g Ground Cumin
- 5 g Salt
- 2 g Black Pepper
- 50 ml Water

Directions

1. Combine olive oil, lime juice, cilantro leaves, minced garlic, ground cumin, salt, and black pepper in a blender.
2. Blend until smooth, adding water gradually to reach desired consistency.
3. Pour the mixture into the slow cooker and set on low for 1 hour to allow flavors to meld.
4. Once done, let it cool and transfer to a jar or bottle for storage.
5. Shake well before serving.

Nutritional Information

Calories: 85, Protein: 0.2g, Carbohydrates: 1g, Fat: 9g, Fiber: 0.2g, Cholesterol: 0 mg, Salt: 150 mg, Potassium: 20 mg

KETO RANCH DIP

Servings 8 | Prep: 10 min | Cook: 0 min

This creamy Keto Ranch Dip is a perfect low-carb condiment, bursting with herbs and tangy flavors. Ideal for dipping veggies or topping your favorite dishes.

Equipment

Mixing Bowl, Whisk, Measuring Spoons

Ingredients

- 240 ml Sour Cream
- 120 ml Mayonnaise
- 10 g Fresh Dill, chopped
- 10 g Fresh Parsley, chopped
- 5 g Garlic Powder
- 5 g Onion Powder
- 2 g Dried Chives
- 5 ml Lemon Juice
- Salt and Pepper to taste

Directions

1. In a mixing bowl, combine sour cream and mayonnaise until smooth.
2. Add fresh dill, parsley, garlic powder, onion powder, and dried chives.
3. Stir in lemon juice, then season with salt and pepper to taste.
4. Whisk all ingredients together until well combined.
5. Refrigerate for at least 30 minutes to allow flavors to meld.

Nutritional Information

Calories: 150, Protein: 1g, Carbohydrates: 2g, Fat: 15g, Fiber: 0g, Cholesterol: 15 mg, Salt: 150 mg, Potassium: 50 mg

SLOW COOKER PESTO SAUCE

This vibrant Slow Cooker Pesto Sauce is a low-carb delight, perfect for enhancing your favorite dishes with a burst of fresh basil and nutty flavors.

Equipment

Slow Cooker, Food Processor, Spatula

Ingredients

- 100 g Fresh Basil Leaves
- 50 g Pine Nuts
- 50 g Parmesan Cheese, grated
- 2 Garlic Cloves
- 120 ml Olive Oil
- 5 g Salt
- 5 g Black Pepper

Directions

1. Place basil leaves, pine nuts, Parmesan cheese, and garlic cloves in a food processor.
2. Pulse until the mixture is finely chopped.
3. Gradually add olive oil while processing until smooth.
4. Transfer the mixture to the slow cooker.
5. Cook on low for 60 minutes, stirring occasionally.
6. Season with salt and black pepper to taste.
7. Allow to cool before storing in an airtight container.

Nutritional Information

Calories: 150, Protein: 3g, Carbohydrates: 2g, Fat: 15g, Fiber: 1g, Cholesterol: 5 mg, Salt: 150 mg, Potassium: 50 mg

SPICY LOW CARB SALSA

This vibrant and zesty salsa is perfect for adding a spicy kick to your meals. Made in a slow cooker, it allows the flavors to meld beautifully, creating a delicious low-carb condiment.

Equipment

Slow Cooker, Cutting Board, Knife

Ingredients

- 500 g tomatoes, chopped
- 100 g red onion, finely diced
- 2 cloves garlic, minced
- 1 jalapeño pepper, seeded and chopped
- 30 ml lime juice
- 10 g fresh cilantro, chopped
- 5 g ground cumin
- 5 g salt
- 2 g black pepper

Directions

1. Place the chopped tomatoes, red onion, garlic, and jalapeño pepper into the slow cooker.
2. Add lime juice, fresh cilantro, ground cumin, salt, and black pepper. Stir well to combine.
3. Cover the slow cooker and set it to low heat. Cook for 2 hours, stirring occasionally.
4. Once cooked, taste and adjust seasoning if necessary.
5. Allow the salsa to cool slightly before serving or storing in an airtight container in the refrigerator.

Nutritional Information

Calories: 25, Protein: 1g, Carbohydrates: 5g, Fat: 0g, Fiber: 1g, Cholesterol: 0 mg, Salt: 150 mg, Potassium: 200 mg

SLOW COOKER CHIPOTLE MAYO

Servings 10 | Prep: 10 min | Cook: 60 min

This creamy and smoky chipotle mayo is the perfect low-carb condiment to elevate your dishes. Made effortlessly in a slow cooker, it adds a spicy kick to sandwiches, salads, and grilled meats.

Equipment

Slow Cooker, Blender, Mixing Bowl

Ingredients

- 200 ml Mayonnaise
- 50 g Chipotle Peppers in Adobo Sauce
- 10 ml Lime Juice
- 5 g Garlic Powder
- 2 g Salt
- 2 g Black Pepper

Directions

1. Place the chipotle peppers in adobo sauce into the slow cooker.
2. Cook on low for 60 minutes to soften and enhance the flavors.
3. Transfer the cooked peppers to a blender. Add mayonnaise, lime juice, garlic powder, salt, and black pepper.
4. Blend until smooth and creamy.
5. Pour the mixture into a mixing bowl and refrigerate for at least 30 minutes before serving to allow flavors to meld.

Nutritional Information

Calories: 100, Protein: 0.5g, Carbohydrates: 1g, Fat: 11g, Fiber: 0.5g, Cholesterol: 5 mg, Salt: 150 mg, Potassium: 20 mg

KETO HORSERADISH CREAM SAUCE

Servings 8 | Prep: 10 min | Cook: 0 min

A creamy, tangy sauce perfect for adding a kick to your favorite dishes, this Keto Horseradish Cream Sauce is both low-carb and full of flavor.

Equipment

Mixing Bowl, Whisk, Measuring Spoons

Ingredients

- 200 ml Sour Cream
- 50 g Prepared Horseradish
- 10 ml Lemon Juice
- 5 g Dijon Mustard
- 2 g Garlic Powder
- 2 g Salt
- 1 g Black Pepper
- 5 g Fresh Chives, chopped

Directions

1. In a mixing bowl, combine the sour cream and prepared horseradish.
2. Add the lemon juice, Dijon mustard, garlic powder, salt, and black pepper.
3. Whisk the mixture until smooth and well combined.
4. Gently fold in the chopped chives.
5. Taste and adjust seasoning if necessary.
6. Transfer to a serving dish or store in an airtight container in the refrigerator until ready to use.

Nutritional Information

Calories: 45, Protein: 1g, Carbohydrates: 2g, Fat: 4g, Fiber: 0g, Cholesterol: 10 mg, Salt: 150 mg, Potassium: 50 mg

SLOW COOKER KETO GRAVY

Servings 8 | Prep: 10 min | Cook: 240 min

This rich and savory keto gravy is perfect for enhancing your favorite low-carb dishes. Made effortlessly in a slow cooker, it delivers deep flavors without the carbs.

Equipment

Slow Cooker, Whisk, Measuring Cups and Spoons

Ingredients

- 500 ml Beef Broth
- 100 g Mushrooms, finely chopped
- 50 g Onion, finely chopped
- 2 cloves Garlic, minced
- 60 ml Heavy Cream
- 30 g Butter
- 5 g Xanthan Gum
- 5 g Fresh Thyme, chopped
- Salt and Pepper to taste

Directions

1. Add the beef broth, mushrooms, onion, and garlic to the slow cooker.
2. Cook on low for 4 hours until the vegetables are tender.
3. Stir in the heavy cream and butter, allowing them to melt and combine.
4. Sprinkle the xanthan gum over the mixture, whisking continuously to avoid clumps.
5. Add fresh thyme, salt, and pepper, adjusting seasoning to taste.
6. Continue to cook for an additional 10 minutes until the gravy thickens.
7. Serve warm over your favorite low-carb dishes.

Nutritional Information

Calories: 80, Protein: 2g, Carbohydrates: 2g, Fat: 7g, Fiber: 0.5g, Cholesterol: 20 mg, Salt: 150 mg, Potassium: 150 mg

LOW CARB CAESAR DRESSING

Servings 8 | Prep: 10 min | Cook: 0 min

This creamy, tangy Caesar dressing is perfect for adding a burst of flavor to your salads without the carbs. Made in a slow cooker, it melds flavors beautifully for a rich, satisfying taste.

Equipment

Blender, Slow Cooker, Measuring Cups and Spoons

Ingredients

- 200 ml Olive Oil
- 50 g Parmesan Cheese, grated
- 2 Anchovy Fillets
- 1 Egg Yolk
- 10 ml Lemon Juice
- 5 g Dijon Mustard
- 2 g Garlic, minced
- 2 g Salt
- 1 g Black Pepper

Directions

1. Combine the egg yolk, lemon juice, Dijon mustard, garlic, salt, and pepper in a blender. Blend until smooth.
2. Slowly drizzle in the olive oil while blending to emulsify the mixture.
3. Add the anchovy fillets and Parmesan cheese, blending until fully incorporated.
4. Transfer the mixture to a slow cooker and set on low for 30 minutes to meld flavors.
5. Allow the dressing to cool before serving. Store in the refrigerator for up to one week.

Nutritional Information

Calories: 180, Protein: 2g, Carbohydrates: 1g, Fat: 19g, Fiber: 0g, Cholesterol: 15 mg, Salt: 150 mg, Potassium: 20 mg

CREAMY JALAPEÑO CHEESE SAUCE

Servings 8 | Prep: 10 min | Cook: 60 min

This creamy jalapeño cheese sauce is the perfect blend of spicy and cheesy, ideal for drizzling over vegetables or using as a dip. Made effortlessly in a slow cooker, it's a low-carb delight that adds a kick to any dish.

Equipment

Slow Cooker, Whisk, Measuring Cups and Spoons

Ingredients

- 250 g cream cheese, cubed
- 200 g cheddar cheese, shredded
- 100 ml heavy cream
- 50 g jalapeños, finely chopped
- 1 clove garlic, minced
- 5 g paprika
- 2 g salt
- 2 g black pepper

Directions

1. Add the cream cheese, cheddar cheese, and heavy cream to the slow cooker.
2. Stir in the chopped jalapeños, minced garlic, paprika, salt, and black pepper.
3. Cover and cook on low for 60 minutes, stirring occasionally until the cheeses are fully melted and the sauce is smooth.
4. Once the sauce is creamy and well combined, taste and adjust seasoning if necessary.
5. Serve warm as a dip or sauce, and enjoy the spicy, cheesy goodness.

Nutritional Information

Calories: 180, Protein: 7g, Carbohydrates: 3g, Fat: 16g, Fiber: 0g, Cholesterol: 45 mg, Salt: 300 mg, Potassium: 80 mg

KETO TERIYAKI SAUCE

Servings 8 | Prep: 10 min | Cook: 60 min

This Keto Teriyaki Sauce is a savory and slightly sweet condiment perfect for enhancing your favorite dishes without the carbs.

Equipment

Slow Cooker, Whisk, Measuring Cups and Spoons

Ingredients

- 120 ml Soy Sauce (or tamari for gluten-free)
- 60 ml Water
- 30 ml Rice Vinegar
- 60 g Erythritol
- 1 clove Garlic, minced
- 1 tsp Ginger, grated
- 1 tsp Sesame Oil
- 1 tsp Xanthan Gum

Directions

1. Combine soy sauce, water, rice vinegar, erythritol, garlic, ginger, and sesame oil in the slow cooker.
2. Whisk the ingredients together until erythritol is dissolved.
3. Cover and cook on low for 60 minutes, stirring occasionally.
4. After cooking, gradually whisk in xanthan gum until the sauce thickens.
5. Allow the sauce to cool before transferring it to a jar for storage.

Nutritional Information

Calories: 10, Protein: 1g, Carbohydrates: 1g, Fat: 0.5g, Fiber: 0g, Cholesterol: 0 mg, Salt: 800 mg, Potassium: 50 mg

SLOW COOKER LOW CARB KETCHUP

Servings 10 | Prep: 10 min | Cook: 240 min

This homemade low carb ketchup is a perfect blend of tangy and sweet flavors, made effortlessly in your slow cooker. It's a healthier alternative to store-bought versions, with no added sugars and all the taste you love.

Equipment

Slow Cooker, Whisk, Measuring Cups and Spoons

Ingredients

- 500 g Tomato Paste
- 250 ml Water
- 60 ml Apple Cider Vinegar
- 50 g Erythritol (or preferred low-carb sweetener)
- 1 tsp Onion Powder
- 1 tsp Garlic Powder
- 1 tsp Smoked Paprika
- 0.5 tsp Salt
- 0.5 tsp Ground Black Pepper
- 0.5 tsp Ground Allspice

Directions

1. In the slow cooker, combine the tomato paste and water, whisking until smooth.
2. Add the apple cider vinegar and erythritol, stirring well to incorporate.
3. Mix in the onion powder, garlic powder, smoked paprika, salt, black pepper, and allspice.
4. Cover and cook on low for 4 hours, stirring occasionally to prevent sticking.
5. Once cooked, allow the ketchup to cool before transferring it to a sterilized jar or bottle for storage.

Nutritional Information

Calories: 20, Protein: 1g, Carbohydrates: 4g, Fat: 0g, Fiber: 1g, Cholesterol: 0 mg, Salt: 120 mg, Potassium: 200 mg

HOMEMADE SUGAR-FREE MAPLE SYRUP

Servings 10 | Prep: 5 min | Cook: 60 min

This sugar-free maple syrup is a delightful, low-carb alternative to traditional maple syrup, perfect for drizzling over pancakes or waffles without the guilt.

Equipment

Slow Cooker, Whisk, Measuring Cups and Spoons

Ingredients

- 500 ml Water
- 200 g Erythritol
- 1 tsp Maple Extract
- 1/2 tsp Xanthan Gum
- 1/4 tsp Salt
- 1/4 tsp Vanilla Extract

Directions

1. Pour the water into the slow cooker and set it to low heat.
2. Add erythritol and whisk until fully dissolved.
3. Stir in the maple extract and salt.
4. Gradually sprinkle in the xanthan gum while whisking continuously to avoid clumps.
5. Cover and let the mixture cook on low for 60 minutes, stirring occasionally.
6. Once thickened to your liking, stir in the vanilla extract.
7. Allow to cool slightly before transferring to a bottle or jar for storage.

Nutritional Information

Calories: 5, Protein: 0g, Carbohydrates: 2g, Fat: 0g, Fiber: 0g, Cholesterol: 0 mg, Salt: 60 mg, Potassium: 0 mg

APPETIZERS AND SNACKS

SLOW COOKER SPINACH ARTICHOKE DIP

Servings 8 | Prep: 10 min | Cook: 120 min

This creamy and savory dip combines the rich flavors of spinach and artichokes, making it a perfect low-carb appetizer for any gathering.

Equipment

Slow Cooker, Mixing Bowl, Spoon

Ingredients

- 250 g Fresh Spinach, chopped
- 200 g Artichoke Hearts, drained and chopped
- 200 g Cream Cheese, softened
- 100 g Sour Cream
- 100 g Grated Parmesan Cheese
- 100 g Shredded Mozzarella Cheese
- 2 cloves Garlic, minced
- 5 g Salt
- 2 g Black Pepper

Directions

1. In a mixing bowl, combine cream cheese, sour cream, Parmesan cheese, mozzarella cheese, garlic, salt, and pepper. Mix until smooth.
2. Add chopped spinach and artichoke hearts to the mixture, stirring until well combined.
3. Transfer the mixture to the slow cooker.
4. Cover and cook on low for 2 hours, stirring occasionally.
5. Once the dip is hot and bubbly, taste and adjust seasoning if necessary.
6. Serve warm with low-carb crackers or vegetable sticks.

Nutritional Information

Calories: 180, Protein: 8g, Carbohydrates: 5g, Fat: 15g, Fiber: 2g, Cholesterol: 35 mg, Salt: 400 mg, Potassium: 150 mg

LOW CARB BACON-WRAPPED JALAPEÑO POPPERS

Servings 8 | Prep: 15 min | Cook: 120 min

These spicy, cheesy jalapeño poppers wrapped in crispy bacon are the perfect low-carb appetizer, offering a delightful blend of heat and savory flavors.

Equipment

Slow Cooker, Mixing Bowl, Knife

Ingredients

- 8 large jalapeños
- 200 g cream cheese
- 100 g shredded cheddar cheese
- 1 clove garlic, minced
- 16 slices bacon
- 1 tsp smoked paprika

Directions

1. Slice the jalapeños in half lengthwise and remove the seeds.
2. In a mixing bowl, combine cream cheese, cheddar cheese, garlic, and smoked paprika.
3. Fill each jalapeño half with the cheese mixture.
4. Wrap each stuffed jalapeño half with a slice of bacon, securing with a toothpick if necessary.
5. Place the bacon-wrapped jalapeños in the slow cooker and cook on low for 2 hours until the bacon is crispy.

Nutritional Information

Calories: 210, Protein: 10g, Carbohydrates: 3g, Fat: 18g, Fiber: 1g, Cholesterol: 40 mg, Salt: 350 mg, Potassium: 150 mg

KETO BUFFALO CAULIFLOWER BITES

Servings 4 | Prep: 10 min | Cook: 120 min

These spicy and tangy cauliflower bites are the perfect low-carb snack, delivering all the flavors of classic buffalo wings without the carbs.

Equipment

Slow Cooker, Mixing Bowl, Whisk

Ingredients

- 500 g Cauliflower, cut into florets
- 100 ml Hot Sauce
- 50 g Unsalted Butter, melted
- 5 g Garlic Powder
- 5 g Onion Powder
- 2 g Paprika
- 2 g Salt
- 1 g Black Pepper

Directions

1. In a mixing bowl, whisk together the hot sauce, melted butter, garlic powder, onion powder, paprika, salt, and black pepper.
2. Add the cauliflower florets to the bowl and toss until they are well coated with the sauce.
3. Transfer the coated cauliflower to the slow cooker.
4. Cover and cook on low for 2 hours, or until the cauliflower is tender.
5. Serve warm, garnished with fresh herbs or a side of low-carb ranch dressing, if desired.

Nutritional Information

Calories: 120, Protein: 3g, Carbohydrates: 5g, Fat: 10g, Fiber: 2g, Cholesterol: 15 mg, Salt: 300 mg, Potassium: 320 mg

PARMESAN GARLIC ZUCCHINI CHIPS

Servings 4 | Prep: 10 min | Cook: 120 min

These crispy Parmesan Garlic Zucchini Chips are a delightful low-carb snack, perfect for satisfying your crunchy cravings without the guilt.

Equipment

Slow Cooker, Mandoline Slicer, Mixing Bowl

Ingredients

- 500 g Zucchini, thinly sliced
- 50 g Parmesan cheese, grated
- 2 cloves Garlic, minced
- 15 ml Olive oil
- 5 g Salt
- 2 g Black pepper

Directions

1. In a mixing bowl, combine zucchini slices, olive oil, minced garlic, salt, and black pepper. Toss until zucchini is well-coated.
2. Layer the zucchini slices in the slow cooker, ensuring they are evenly spread out.
3. Sprinkle grated Parmesan cheese evenly over the zucchini slices.
4. Cover the slow cooker with a lid and set it to low heat. Cook for 2 hours or until the zucchini chips are crispy.
5. Once done, remove the chips from the slow cooker and let them cool on a wire rack for a few minutes before serving.

Nutritional Information

Calories: 110, Protein: 6g, Carbohydrates: 4g, Fat: 8g, Fiber: 1g, Cholesterol: 10 mg, Salt: 300 mg, Potassium: 350 mg

SLOW COOKER CHEESE FONDUE

Servings 6 | Prep: 10 min | Cook: 90 min

Indulge in a creamy and savory cheese fondue, perfect for dipping low-carb vegetables or meats. This slow cooker recipe ensures a smooth and flavorful fondue with minimal effort.

Equipment

Slow Cooker, Whisk, Serving Dish

Ingredients

- 500 g Gruyère cheese, shredded
- 250 g Emmental cheese, shredded
- 250 ml dry white wine
- 2 cloves garlic, minced
- 5 g Dijon mustard
- 5 g lemon juice
- 2 g ground nutmeg
- Salt and pepper to taste

Directions

1. Add the shredded Gruyère and Emmental cheeses to the slow cooker.
2. Pour in the dry white wine and add the minced garlic.
3. Stir in the Dijon mustard, lemon juice, and ground nutmeg.
4. Cover and cook on low for 90 minutes, stirring occasionally until the cheese is melted and smooth.
5. Season with salt and pepper to taste before serving.

Nutritional Information

Calories: 350, Protein: 20g, Carbohydrates: 2g, Fat: 28g, Fiber: 0g, Cholesterol: 80 mg, Salt: 400 mg, Potassium: 100 mg

SPICY ROASTED CHICKPEAS

Servings 4 | Prep: 10 min | Cook: 240 min

These spicy roasted chickpeas are a crunchy, flavorful snack that's perfect for any occasion. The slow cooker method ensures they are perfectly roasted with a delightful kick.

Equipment

Slow Cooker, Mixing Bowl, Baking Sheet

Ingredients

- 400 g Canned Chickpeas, drained and rinsed
- 15 ml Olive Oil
- 5 g Paprika
- 5 g Garlic Powder
- 3 g Cayenne Pepper
- 3 g Salt
- 2 g Black Pepper

Directions

1. Preheat the slow cooker on high.
2. In a mixing bowl, combine chickpeas, olive oil, paprika, garlic powder, cayenne pepper, salt, and black pepper. Mix well to coat the chickpeas evenly.
3. Spread the seasoned chickpeas in a single layer on a baking sheet.
4. Transfer the chickpeas to the slow cooker. Cover and cook on high for 4 hours, stirring occasionally.
5. Once done, spread the chickpeas back on the baking sheet to cool and crisp up.
6. Serve warm or store in an airtight container for up to a week.

Nutritional Information

Calories: 120, Protein: 6g, Carbohydrates: 18g, Fat: 4g, Fiber: 5g, Cholesterol: 0 mg, Salt: 300 mg, Potassium: 200 mg

KETO MOZZARELLA STICKS

Indulge in these crispy, cheesy keto mozzarella sticks, perfect for a low-carb snack or appetizer. Made effortlessly in a slow cooker, they offer a delightful crunch with every bite.

Equipment

Slow Cooker, Mixing Bowl, Baking Sheet

Ingredients

- 200 g Mozzarella Cheese, cut into sticks
- 100 g Almond Flour
- 2 Large Eggs, beaten
- 50 g Grated Parmesan Cheese
- 5 g Garlic Powder
- 5 g Italian Seasoning
- 2 g Salt
- 2 g Black Pepper
- 50 ml Olive Oil

Directions

1. In a mixing bowl, combine almond flour, Parmesan cheese, garlic powder, Italian seasoning, salt, and black pepper.
2. Dip each mozzarella stick into the beaten eggs, then coat with the almond flour mixture. Repeat to ensure a thick coating.
3. Place the coated mozzarella sticks on a baking sheet and freeze for 30 minutes to set.
4. Preheat the slow cooker and add olive oil to the bottom.
5. Arrange the frozen mozzarella sticks in the slow cooker, ensuring they do not overlap.
6. Cook on low for 60 minutes or until golden brown and crispy.
7. Serve immediately with your favorite low-carb dipping sauce.

Nutritional Information

Calories: 320, Protein: 18g, Carbohydrates: 5g, Fat: 26g, Fiber: 2g, Cholesterol: 80 mg, Salt: 300 mg, Potassium: 150 mg

BBQ CHICKEN DIP

This creamy and savory BBQ Chicken Dip is a perfect low-carb appetizer, combining tender chicken with a smoky barbecue flavor, all made effortlessly in your slow cooker.

Equipment

Slow Cooker, Mixing Bowl, Spoon

Ingredients

- 500 g boneless, skinless chicken breasts
- 200 g cream cheese, softened
- 150 ml sugar-free BBQ sauce
- 100 g shredded cheddar cheese
- 50 g chopped green onions
- 1 tsp garlic powder
- 1 tsp smoked paprika
- Salt and pepper to taste

Directions

1. Place the chicken breasts in the slow cooker and season with garlic powder, smoked paprika, salt, and pepper.
2. Add the cream cheese and BBQ sauce over the chicken.
3. Cover and cook on low for 2 hours, or until the chicken is fully cooked and tender.
4. Shred the chicken using two forks, then stir in the shredded cheddar cheese and chopped green onions.
5. Mix well until the cheese is melted and everything is combined.
6. Serve warm with low-carb crackers or vegetable sticks.

Nutritional Information

Calories: 280, Protein: 25g, Carbohydrates: 5g, Fat: 18g, Fiber: 1g, Cholesterol: 80 mg, Salt: 600 mg, Potassium: 350 mg

SLOW COOKER KETO NACHOS

Servings 4 | Prep: 15 min | Cook: 120 min

These Slow Cooker Keto Nachos are a delicious low-carb twist on a classic favorite. Perfect for a snack or appetizer, they are loaded with flavor and easy to prepare.

Equipment

Slow Cooker, Mixing Bowl, Serving Platter

Ingredients

- 500 g ground beef
- 150 g cheddar cheese, shredded
- 100 g bell peppers, sliced
- 100 g onions, diced
- 50 g jalapeños, sliced
- 200 g cauliflower florets
- 30 ml olive oil
- 5 g taco seasoning
- 5 g salt
- 5 g black pepper

Directions

1. Heat olive oil in a pan over medium heat and brown the ground beef.
2. Add taco seasoning, salt, and pepper to the beef, stirring well.
3. Place cauliflower florets at the bottom of the slow cooker.
4. Layer the cooked beef, bell peppers, onions, and jalapeños over the cauliflower.
5. Top with shredded cheddar cheese.
6. Cover and cook on low for 2 hours.
7. Serve hot on a platter and enjoy your keto nachos!

Nutritional Information

Calories: 450, Protein: 30g, Carbohydrates: 8g, Fat: 35g, Fiber: 3g, Cholesterol: 90 mg, Salt: 600 mg, Potassium: 700 mg

SLOW COOKER PEPPERONI CHIPS

Servings 4 | Prep: 5 min | Cook: 120 min

These crispy, savory pepperoni chips are the perfect low-carb snack, offering a delightful crunch with every bite. Ideal for parties or a quick snack, they are effortlessly made in a slow cooker.

Equipment

Slow Cooker, Parchment Paper, Kitchen Scissors

Ingredients

- 200 g Pepperoni Slices
- 1 g Paprika
- 1 g Garlic Powder
- 1 g Dried Oregano

Directions

1. Line the slow cooker with parchment paper to prevent sticking.
2. Arrange the pepperoni slices in a single layer at the bottom of the slow cooker.
3. Sprinkle paprika, garlic powder, and dried oregano evenly over the pepperoni slices.
4. Cover the slow cooker with the lid slightly ajar to allow moisture to escape.
5. Cook on low for 2 hours or until the pepperoni slices are crispy.
6. Remove the chips and let them cool on a paper towel to absorb excess oil.

Nutritional Information

Calories: 150, Protein: 6g, Carbohydrates: 1g, Fat: 13g, Fiber: 0g, Cholesterol: 30mg, Salt: 500mg, Potassium: 100mg

SPICY SAUSAGE-STUFFED MUSHROOMS

Servings 6 | Prep: 15 min | Cook: 120 min

These Spicy Sausage-Stuffed Mushrooms are a delightful low-carb appetizer, combining the earthy flavor of mushrooms with a spicy sausage kick, all slow-cooked to perfection.

Equipment

Slow Cooker, Mixing Bowl, Spoon

Ingredients

- 500 g button mushrooms, stems removed
- 250 g spicy Italian sausage, casing removed
- 100 g cream cheese, softened
- 50 g grated Parmesan cheese
- 1 clove garlic, minced
- 5 g fresh parsley, chopped
- 2 g black pepper
- 2 g salt

Directions

1. In a mixing bowl, combine the sausage, cream cheese, Parmesan, garlic, parsley, black pepper, and salt until well mixed.
2. Stuff each mushroom cap with the sausage mixture, pressing gently to fill.
3. Place the stuffed mushrooms in the slow cooker in a single layer.
4. Cover and cook on low for 2 hours, or until the mushrooms are tender and the filling is cooked through.
5. Serve warm, garnished with additional parsley if desired.

Nutritional Information

Calories: 180, Protein: 12g, Carbohydrates: 4g, Fat: 14g, Fiber: 1g, Cholesterol: 40 mg, Salt: 320 mg, Potassium: 350 mg

GARLIC PARMESAN WINGS

Servings 4 | Prep: 10 min | Cook: 180 min

These Garlic Parmesan Wings are a savory delight, perfect for a low-carb snack or appetizer. The slow cooker ensures the wings are tender, while a quick broil gives them a crispy finish.

Equipment

Slow Cooker, Baking Sheet, Broiler

Ingredients

- 1 kg Chicken Wings
- 60 ml Olive Oil
- 4 cloves Garlic, minced
- 50 g Parmesan Cheese, grated
- 5 g Dried Oregano
- 5 g Salt
- 3 g Black Pepper
- 10 g Fresh Parsley, chopped

Directions

1. In a bowl, combine olive oil, minced garlic, oregano, salt, and pepper.
2. Toss the chicken wings in the mixture until well coated.
3. Place the wings in the slow cooker and cook on low for 3 hours.
4. Preheat the broiler. Transfer the wings to a baking sheet and sprinkle with Parmesan cheese.
5. Broil for 5 minutes or until the wings are golden and crispy.
6. Garnish with fresh parsley before serving.

Nutritional Information

Calories: 420, Protein: 35g, Carbohydrates: 2g, Fat: 30g, Fiber: 0g, Cholesterol: 120 mg, Salt: 500 mg, Potassium: 300 mg

CRISPY COCONUT SHRIMP

This crispy coconut shrimp is a delightful low-carb appetizer, offering a perfect balance of savory and sweet flavors with a satisfying crunch.

Equipment

Slow Cooker, Mixing Bowl, Baking Sheet

Ingredients

- 500 g large shrimp, peeled and deveined
- 100 g unsweetened shredded coconut
- 50 g almond flour
- 2 large eggs
- 5 g garlic powder
- 5 g paprika
- 2 g salt
- 2 g black pepper
- 30 ml coconut oil, melted

Directions

1. In a mixing bowl, combine the shredded coconut, almond flour, garlic powder, paprika, salt, and black pepper.
2. In a separate bowl, beat the eggs.
3. Dip each shrimp into the egg mixture, then coat with the coconut mixture, pressing gently to adhere.
4. Place the coated shrimp on a baking sheet lined with parchment paper.
5. Drizzle the melted coconut oil over the shrimp.
6. Transfer the shrimp to the slow cooker, cover, and cook on low for 2 hours or until crispy and cooked through.

Nutritional Information

Calories: 320, Protein: 25g, Carbohydrates: 8g, Fat: 22g, Fiber: 4g, Cholesterol: 215 mg, Salt: 400 mg, Potassium: 350 mg

KETO DEVILED EGGS

A classic appetizer with a keto twist, these deviled eggs are creamy, tangy, and perfect for any low-carb gathering.

Equipment

Mixing Bowl, Spoon, Knife

Ingredients

- 6 large eggs, hard-boiled and peeled
- 60 g mayonnaise
- 10 g Dijon mustard
- 5 g apple cider vinegar
- 2 g paprika
- Salt and pepper to taste
- 10 g fresh chives, chopped

Directions

1. Slice the hard-boiled eggs in half lengthwise and remove the yolks.
2. In a mixing bowl, mash the yolks with a fork.
3. Add mayonnaise, Dijon mustard, apple cider vinegar, salt, and pepper to the yolks. Mix until smooth.
4. Spoon or pipe the yolk mixture back into the egg whites.
5. Garnish with paprika and chopped chives.

Nutritional Information

Calories: 120, Protein: 6g, Carbohydrates: 1g, Fat: 10g, Fiber: 0g, Cholesterol: 190 mg, Salt: 150 mg, Potassium: 60 mg

SLOW COOKER JALAPEÑO CHEESE DIP

Servings 8 | Prep: 10 min | Cook: 120 min

This creamy, spicy jalapeño cheese dip is perfect for any gathering. The slow cooker melds the flavors beautifully, creating a rich and satisfying appetizer that pairs perfectly with low-carb dippers.

Equipment

Slow Cooker, Mixing Bowl, Spatula

Ingredients

- 250 g Cream Cheese, cubed
- 200 g Cheddar Cheese, shredded
- 100 g Jalapeños, sliced
- 100 ml Heavy Cream
- 50 g Diced Tomatoes, drained
- 1 tsp Garlic Powder
- 1 tsp Onion Powder
- 1/2 tsp Salt
- 1/4 tsp Black Pepper

Directions

1. Place the cream cheese, cheddar cheese, jalapeños, heavy cream, and diced tomatoes into the slow cooker.
2. Sprinkle the garlic powder, onion powder, salt, and black pepper over the ingredients.
3. Stir everything together until well combined.
4. Cover and cook on low for 2 hours, stirring occasionally to ensure even melting.
5. Once the cheese is fully melted and the dip is smooth, give it a final stir and serve warm.

Nutritional Information

Calories: 210, Protein: 8g, Carbohydrates: 4g, Fat: 18g, Fiber: 1g, Cholesterol: 50 mg, Salt: 400 mg, Potassium: 150 mg

BACON AND EGG FAT BOMBS

Servings 8 | Prep: 10 min | Cook: 60 min

Indulge in these savory, low-carb bacon and egg fat bombs, perfect for a satisfying snack or appetizer. The creamy texture and rich flavors make them irresistible.

Equipment

Slow Cooker, Mixing Bowl, Spoon

Ingredients

- 200 g Bacon, chopped
- 6 Large Eggs
- 100 g Cream Cheese, softened
- 50 g Cheddar Cheese, shredded
- 30 ml Heavy Cream
- 5 g Garlic Powder
- 5 g Onion Powder
- Salt and Pepper to taste

Directions

1. Preheat the slow cooker on low setting.
2. In a mixing bowl, whisk together the eggs, cream cheese, heavy cream, garlic powder, onion powder, salt, and pepper until smooth.
3. Stir in the chopped bacon and shredded cheddar cheese.
4. Pour the mixture into the slow cooker, spreading it evenly.
5. Cover and cook on low for 60 minutes, or until the mixture is set and firm.
6. Allow to cool slightly, then cut into bite-sized pieces.
7. Serve warm or store in the refrigerator for later.

Nutritional Information

Calories: 180, Protein: 10g, Carbohydrates: 2g, Fat: 15g, Fiber: 0g, Cholesterol: 120 mg, Salt: 350 mg, Potassium: 150 mg

KETO SAUSAGE BALLS

These savory keto sausage balls are the perfect low-carb appetizer or snack, packed with flavor and easy to make in your slow cooker.

Equipment

Slow Cooker, Mixing Bowl, Measuring Cups

Ingredients

- 500 g Ground Pork Sausage
- 150 g Almond Flour
- 100 g Cheddar Cheese, shredded
- 2 Large Eggs
- 5 g Baking Powder
- 2 g Garlic Powder
- 2 g Onion Powder
- 2 g Salt
- 1 g Black Pepper

Directions

1. In a mixing bowl, combine the ground pork sausage, almond flour, and shredded cheddar cheese.
2. Add the eggs, baking powder, garlic powder, onion powder, salt, and black pepper to the mixture. Mix until well combined.
3. Form the mixture into small balls, about 2.5 cm in diameter.
4. Place the sausage balls in the slow cooker, ensuring they are in a single layer.
5. Cover and cook on low for 3 hours, or until the sausage balls are cooked through and golden brown.

Nutritional Information

Calories: 250, Protein: 18g, Carbohydrates: 3g, Fat: 20g, Fiber: 1g, Cholesterol: 80 mg, Salt: 450 mg, Potassium: 220 mg

KETO-FRIENDLY SMOKED SALMON BITES

These delightful smoked salmon bites are perfect for a low-carb appetizer, combining creamy cheese and savory salmon for a satisfying snack.

Equipment

Slow Cooker, Mixing Bowl, Serving Platter

Ingredients

- 200 g smoked salmon, thinly sliced
- 150 g cream cheese, softened
- 50 g cucumber, finely diced
- 30 ml lemon juice
- 10 g fresh dill, chopped
- 5 g capers, drained
- Salt and pepper to taste

Directions

1. In a mixing bowl, combine cream cheese, lemon juice, dill, and a pinch of salt and pepper. Mix until smooth.
2. Lay out the smoked salmon slices on a flat surface.
3. Spread a thin layer of the cream cheese mixture onto each slice of salmon.
4. Sprinkle diced cucumber and capers evenly over the cream cheese layer.
5. Roll each salmon slice into a bite-sized roll and secure with a toothpick if necessary.
6. Place the salmon bites in the slow cooker, cover, and cook on low for 60 minutes to allow flavors to meld.
7. Serve warm on a platter, garnished with extra dill if desired.

Nutritional Information

Calories: 85, Protein: 6g, Carbohydrates: 2g, Fat: 6g, Fiber: 0g, Cholesterol: 20mg, Salt: 200mg, Potassium: 150mg

SLOW COOKER ALMOND BUTTER CUPS

Servings 12 | Prep: 15 min | Cook: 60 min

Indulge in these rich and creamy almond butter cups, a perfect low-carb treat made effortlessly in your slow cooker.

Equipment

Slow Cooker, Silicone Muffin Cups, Mixing Bowl

Ingredients

- 200 g Dark Chocolate (85% cocoa or higher)
- 120 g Almond Butter
- 30 g Coconut Oil
- 5 ml Vanilla Extract
- 2 g Sea Salt

Directions

1. Break the dark chocolate into small pieces and place them in a mixing bowl.
2. Add the almond butter and coconut oil to the bowl, then stir in the vanilla extract and sea salt.
3. Pour the mixture into silicone muffin cups, filling each about halfway.
4. Arrange the cups in the slow cooker, cover, and cook on low for 60 minutes until the chocolate is melted and smooth.
5. Carefully remove the cups from the slow cooker and let them cool at room temperature before refrigerating until set.

Nutritional Information

Calories: 150, Protein: 3g, Carbohydrates: 5g, Fat: 13g, Fiber: 3g, Cholesterol: 0 mg, Salt: 50 mg, Potassium: 150 mg

LOW CARB HERB CRACKERS

Servings 6 | Prep: 15 min | Cook: 120 min

These crispy, flavorful herb crackers are perfect for snacking or serving as an appetizer. Made with almond flour and a blend of herbs, they are both low in carbs and high in taste.

Equipment

Slow Cooker, Mixing Bowl, Parchment Paper

Ingredients

- 200 g almond flour
- 50 g grated Parmesan cheese
- 1 tsp dried rosemary
- 1 tsp dried thyme
- 1/2 tsp garlic powder
- 1/2 tsp salt
- 1/4 tsp black pepper
- 1 large egg
- 30 ml olive oil

Directions

1. In a mixing bowl, combine almond flour, Parmesan cheese, rosemary, thyme, garlic powder, salt, and black pepper.
2. Add the egg and olive oil to the dry ingredients and mix until a dough forms.
3. Roll out the dough between two sheets of parchment paper to about 3 mm thickness.
4. Cut the dough into cracker-sized pieces and place them on a parchment-lined slow cooker.
5. Cover and cook on low for 2 hours or until the crackers are golden and crisp.

Nutritional Information

Calories: 180, Protein: 7g, Carbohydrates: 4g, Fat: 16g, Fiber: 2g, Cholesterol: 25 mg, Salt: 150 mg, Potassium: 50 mg

DESSERTS

SLOW COOKER KETO CHOCOLATE LAVA CAKE

Servings 6 | Prep: 15 min | Cook: 120 min

Indulge in a rich, gooey chocolate lava cake that's low in carbs and perfect for keto enthusiasts. This slow cooker dessert is a delightful treat that satisfies your sweet tooth without the guilt.

Equipment

Slow Cooker, Mixing Bowl, Whisk

Ingredients

- 200g Dark Chocolate (85% cocoa or higher)
- 100g Unsalted Butter
- 100ml Heavy Cream
- 3 Large Eggs
- 100g Erythritol
- 50g Almond Flour
- 1 tsp Vanilla Extract
- 1/2 tsp Baking Powder
- Pinch of Salt

Directions

1. Melt the dark chocolate and butter together in a microwave or double boiler until smooth.
2. In a mixing bowl, whisk together the eggs, erythritol, and vanilla extract until well combined.
3. Gradually add the melted chocolate mixture to the egg mixture, stirring continuously.
4. Fold in the almond flour, baking powder, and salt until the batter is smooth.
5. Grease the slow cooker with a bit of butter and pour the batter in.
6. Cover and cook on low for 2 hours or until the edges are set but the center remains gooey.
7. Let it cool slightly before serving warm.

Nutritional Information

Calories: 320, Protein: 6g, Carbohydrates: 8g, Fat: 30g, Fiber: 4g, Cholesterol: 110mg, Salt: 50mg, Potassium: 220mg

LOW CARB CHEESECAKE BITES

Servings 12 | Prep: 15 min | Cook: 120 min

Indulge in these creamy, low-carb cheesecake bites, perfect for satisfying your sweet tooth without the guilt. Made effortlessly in a slow cooker, these bites are a delightful treat for any occasion.

Equipment

Slow Cooker, Mixing Bowl, Muffin Tin

Ingredients

- 400 g Cream Cheese, softened
- 100 g Erythritol
- 2 large Eggs
- 5 ml Vanilla Extract
- 100 ml Heavy Cream
- 50 g Almond Flour
- 30 g Butter, melted

Directions

1. In a mixing bowl, combine almond flour and melted butter. Press the mixture into the bottom of each muffin tin to form a crust.
2. In another bowl, beat the cream cheese and erythritol until smooth. Add eggs one at a time, mixing well after each addition.
3. Stir in vanilla extract and heavy cream until fully incorporated.
4. Pour the cream cheese mixture over the crust in each muffin tin.
5. Place the muffin tin in the slow cooker. Add enough water to the slow cooker to reach halfway up the sides of the muffin tin.
6. Cover and cook on low for 2 hours, or until the cheesecake bites are set.
7. Allow to cool before refrigerating for at least 2 hours before serving.

Nutritional Information

Calories: 180, Protein: 4g, Carbohydrates: 3g, Fat: 17g, Fiber: 1g, Cholesterol: 60 mg, Salt: 120 mg, Potassium: 50 mg

SLOW COOKER PUMPKIN CUSTARD

Servings 6 | Prep: 10 min | Cook: 180 min

Indulge in the creamy, spiced delight of pumpkin custard, effortlessly prepared in your slow cooker. This low-carb dessert is perfect for cozy evenings and festive gatherings.

Equipment

Slow Cooker, Mixing Bowl, Whisk

Ingredients

- 500 g pumpkin puree
- 240 ml heavy cream
- 3 large eggs
- 100 g erythritol (or preferred low-carb sweetener)
- 5 ml vanilla extract
- 5 g ground cinnamon
- 2 g ground nutmeg
- 1 g ground ginger
- 1 g ground cloves

Directions

1. In a mixing bowl, whisk together the pumpkin puree, heavy cream, and eggs until smooth.
2. Add erythritol, vanilla extract, cinnamon, nutmeg, ginger, and cloves to the mixture, and whisk until well combined.
3. Pour the mixture into the slow cooker, spreading it evenly.
4. Cover and cook on low for 3 hours, or until the custard is set and a knife inserted in the center comes out clean.
5. Allow to cool slightly before serving. Enjoy warm or chilled.

Nutritional Information

Calories: 180, Protein: 4g, Carbohydrates: 8g, Fat: 16g, Fiber: 2g, Cholesterol: 110 mg, Salt: 50 mg, Potassium: 250 mg

SUGAR-FREE PEANUT BUTTER FUDGE

Servings 12 | Prep: 10 min | Cook: 120 min

Indulge in this creamy, rich peanut butter fudge without the guilt. Perfectly sweetened without sugar, it's a delightful low-carb treat.

Equipment

Slow Cooker, Mixing Bowl, Spatula

Ingredients

- 250 g Natural Peanut Butter
- 100 g Cream Cheese, softened
- 60 ml Heavy Cream
- 50 g Erythritol
- 1 tsp Vanilla Extract
- 1/4 tsp Salt

Directions

1. In a mixing bowl, combine the peanut butter, cream cheese, heavy cream, erythritol, vanilla extract, and salt until smooth.
2. Transfer the mixture to the slow cooker and spread evenly.
3. Set the slow cooker to low and cook for 2 hours, stirring occasionally.
4. Once the mixture is thick and creamy, pour it into a lined baking dish.
5. Allow the fudge to cool and set in the refrigerator for at least 2 hours before slicing.

Nutritional Information

Calories: 180, Protein: 5g, Carbohydrates: 4g, Fat: 16g, Fiber: 2g, Cholesterol: 15 mg, Salt: 120 mg, Potassium: 150 mg

KETO VANILLA PUDDING

Servings 4 | Prep: 10 min | Cook: 120 min

Indulge in a creamy, low-carb delight with this Keto Vanilla Pudding. Perfectly sweetened and velvety smooth, it's a guilt-free dessert that satisfies your sweet tooth.

Equipment

Slow Cooker, Whisk, Mixing Bowl

Ingredients

- 500 ml Heavy Cream
- 100 ml Unsweetened Almond Milk
- 50 g Erythritol
- 1 tsp Vanilla Extract
- 3 Egg Yolks
- 1 g Xanthan Gum

Directions

1. In a mixing bowl, whisk together the heavy cream, almond milk, erythritol, and vanilla extract until well combined.
2. In a separate bowl, lightly beat the egg yolks. Slowly add them to the cream mixture, whisking continuously.
3. Pour the mixture into the slow cooker and set it to low heat.
4. Cook for 2 hours, stirring occasionally to ensure even cooking.
5. After 2 hours, sprinkle in the xanthan gum and whisk until the pudding thickens.
6. Allow the pudding to cool slightly before serving or refrigerate for a chilled version.

Nutritional Information

Calories: 320, Protein: 4g, Carbohydrates: 4g, Fat: 32g, Fiber: 0g, Cholesterol: 180 mg, Salt: 50 mg, Potassium: 100 mg

SLOW COOKER CINNAMON ALMOND CAKE

Servings 8 | Prep: 15 min | Cook: 120 min

Indulge in the warm, comforting flavors of cinnamon and almond with this low-carb cake, perfectly baked in a slow cooker for a moist and tender crumb.

Equipment

Slow Cooker, Mixing Bowl, Whisk

Ingredients

- 200 g Almond Flour
- 100 g Erythritol
- 5 g Baking Powder
- 5 g Ground Cinnamon
- 3 Large Eggs
- 100 ml Unsweetened Almond Milk
- 60 ml Coconut Oil, melted
- 5 ml Vanilla Extract
- 50 g Sliced Almonds

Directions

1. In a mixing bowl, whisk together almond flour, erythritol, baking powder, and ground cinnamon.
2. In another bowl, beat the eggs, then add almond milk, melted coconut oil, and vanilla extract. Mix well.
3. Combine the wet and dry ingredients, stirring until a smooth batter forms.
4. Grease the slow cooker with a bit of coconut oil and pour in the batter.
5. Sprinkle sliced almonds evenly over the top.
6. Cover and cook on low for 2 hours, or until a toothpick inserted in the center comes out clean.
7. Allow the cake to cool slightly before serving.

Nutritional Information

Calories: 210, Protein: 7g, Carbohydrates: 5g, Fat: 18g, Fiber: 3g, Cholesterol: 55 mg, Salt: 50 mg, Potassium: 120 mg

KETO COCONUT MACAROONS

Indulge in these delightful keto coconut macaroons, perfectly sweetened and low in carbs, making them an ideal guilt-free dessert.

Equipment

Slow Cooker, Mixing Bowl, Baking Sheet

Ingredients

- 200 g Unsweetened Shredded Coconut
- 100 g Almond Flour
- 100 ml Coconut Milk
- 50 g Erythritol
- 2 Large Eggs
- 1 tsp Vanilla Extract
- 1/4 tsp Salt

Directions

1. In a mixing bowl, combine shredded coconut, almond flour, and erythritol.
2. Add coconut milk, eggs, vanilla extract, and salt to the dry ingredients. Mix until well combined.
3. Shape the mixture into small balls and place them on a baking sheet lined with parchment paper.
4. Transfer the baking sheet to the slow cooker. Cover and cook on low for 2 hours.
5. Allow the macaroons to cool before serving.

Nutritional Information

Calories: 120, Protein: 3g, Carbohydrates: 4g, Fat: 10g, Fiber: 2g, Cholesterol: 20 mg, Salt: 50 mg, Potassium: 60 mg

LOW CARB CHOCOLATE CHIP COOKIES

Indulge in these rich, low-carb chocolate chip cookies, perfectly crafted in a slow cooker for a soft, chewy texture that satisfies your sweet tooth without the guilt.

Equipment

Slow Cooker, Mixing Bowl, Parchment Paper

Ingredients

- 200 g Almond Flour
- 100 g Erythritol
- 100 g Sugar-Free Dark Chocolate Chips
- 100 g Unsalted Butter, melted
- 1 Large Egg
- 5 ml Vanilla Extract
- 2 g Baking Powder
- 1 g Salt

Directions

1. Line the slow cooker with parchment paper to prevent sticking.
2. In a mixing bowl, combine almond flour, erythritol, baking powder, and salt.
3. Stir in melted butter, egg, and vanilla extract until a dough forms.
4. Fold in the chocolate chips evenly throughout the dough.
5. Shape the dough into small balls and place them on the parchment paper inside the slow cooker.
6. Cover and cook on low for 2 hours, or until the cookies are set and slightly golden.
7. Allow to cool before serving.

Nutritional Information

Calories: 150, Protein: 4g, Carbohydrates: 5g, Fat: 13g, Fiber: 2g, Cholesterol: 20 mg, Salt: 50 mg, Potassium: 50 mg

SLOW COOKER STRAWBERRY SHORTCAKE

Indulge in a delightful low-carb dessert with this Slow Cooker Strawberry Shortcake. Juicy strawberries and a tender almond flour cake come together for a guilt-free treat.

Equipment

Slow Cooker, Mixing Bowl, Whisk

Ingredients

- 300 g Fresh Strawberries, sliced
- 100 g Almond Flour
- 50 g Coconut Flour
- 100 g Erythritol
- 2 Large Eggs
- 100 ml Unsweetened Almond Milk
- 50 g Butter, melted
- 1 tsp Baking Powder
- 1 tsp Vanilla Extract

Directions

1. In a mixing bowl, whisk together almond flour, coconut flour, erythritol, and baking powder.
2. Add eggs, almond milk, melted butter, and vanilla extract to the dry ingredients. Mix until smooth.
3. Grease the slow cooker with a bit of butter and pour the batter into it.
4. Spread sliced strawberries evenly over the batter.
5. Cover and cook on low for 2 hours or until the cake is set and a toothpick comes out clean.
6. Let it cool slightly before serving.

Nutritional Information

Calories: 210, Protein: 6g, Carbohydrates: 10g, Fat: 16g, Fiber: 4g, Cholesterol: 60 mg, Salt: 120 mg, Potassium: 150 mg

KETO-FRIENDLY LEMON BARS

These zesty and refreshing lemon bars are a perfect low-carb treat, combining the tangy flavor of lemons with a buttery almond crust. Ideal for a guilt-free dessert or a sweet snack.

Equipment

Slow Cooker, Mixing Bowl, Whisk, Baking Dish

Ingredients

- 200 g Almond Flour
- 100 g Unsalted Butter, melted
- 50 g Erythritol
- 3 Large Eggs
- 120 ml Fresh Lemon Juice
- 1 tsp Lemon Zest
- 1 tsp Vanilla Extract
- 1/2 tsp Baking Powder
- Pinch of Salt

Directions

1. In a mixing bowl, combine almond flour, 50 g of erythritol, and melted butter. Mix until crumbly.
2. Press the almond mixture into the bottom of a greased baking dish to form the crust.
3. In another bowl, whisk together eggs, lemon juice, lemon zest, vanilla extract, baking powder, and a pinch of salt until smooth.
4. Pour the lemon mixture over the crust in the baking dish.
5. Place the baking dish in the slow cooker. Cover and cook on low for 2 hours, or until the lemon filling is set.
6. Allow to cool before slicing into bars.

Nutritional Information

Calories: 210, Protein: 6g, Carbohydrates: 5g, Fat: 18g, Fiber: 3g, Cholesterol: 70 mg, Salt: 60 mg, Potassium: 80 mg

SLOW COOKER CHOCOLATE PEANUT BUTTER MOUSSE

Servings 4 | Prep: 10 min | Cook: 120 min

Indulge in a rich and creamy low-carb dessert with this Slow Cooker Chocolate Peanut Butter Mousse. It's a delightful treat that combines the classic flavors of chocolate and peanut butter, all while being easy to prepare in your slow cooker.

Equipment

Slow Cooker, Mixing Bowl, Whisk

Ingredients

- 200 g Dark Chocolate (70% cocoa or higher)
- 100 ml Heavy Cream
- 100 g Cream Cheese, softened
- 50 g Peanut Butter (unsweetened)
- 50 ml Almond Milk
- 2 tbsp Erythritol (or preferred low-carb sweetener)
- 1 tsp Vanilla Extract

Directions

1. Break the dark chocolate into small pieces and place them in the slow cooker.
2. Add the heavy cream and almond milk to the slow cooker. Stir gently to combine.
3. Set the slow cooker to low heat and cook for about 1 hour, stirring occasionally until the chocolate is fully melted and smooth.
4. In a mixing bowl, whisk together the cream cheese, peanut butter, erythritol, and vanilla extract until smooth.
5. Gradually add the melted chocolate mixture to the cream cheese mixture, whisking continuously until fully combined.
6. Pour the mousse mixture back into the slow cooker and cook on low for an additional 1 hour, stirring occasionally.
7. Once thickened, transfer the mousse to serving dishes and refrigerate for at least 1 hour before serving.

Nutritional Information

Calories: 350, Protein: 7g, Carbohydrates: 8g, Fat: 30g, Fiber: 4g, Cholesterol: 45 mg, Salt: 100 mg, Potassium: 250 mg

LOW CARB RASPBERRY CRUMBLE

Servings 6 | Prep: 10 min | Cook: 120 min

Indulge in a delightful low-carb dessert with this Raspberry Crumble, perfectly crafted in a slow cooker. The tartness of raspberries combined with a nutty almond topping makes for a guilt-free treat.

Equipment

Slow Cooker, Mixing Bowl, Spatula

Ingredients

- 500 g Fresh Raspberries
- 100 g Almond Flour
- 50 g Unsweetened Shredded Coconut
- 50 g Butter, melted
- 30 g Erythritol or preferred low-carb sweetener
- 5 ml Vanilla Extract
- 2 g Ground Cinnamon
- 1 g Salt

Directions

1. In a mixing bowl, combine almond flour, shredded coconut, erythritol, melted butter, vanilla extract, ground cinnamon, and salt. Mix until crumbly.
2. Place the raspberries evenly at the bottom of the slow cooker.
3. Sprinkle the crumble mixture over the raspberries, ensuring an even layer.
4. Cover and cook on low for 2 hours or until the topping is golden and the raspberries are bubbly.
5. Allow to cool slightly before serving.

Nutritional Information

Calories: 180, Protein: 4g, Carbohydrates: 10g, Fat: 15g, Fiber: 5g, Cholesterol: 15 mg, Salt: 50 mg, Potassium: 150 mg

KETO CHURRO BITES

Indulge in these delightful Keto Churro Bites, a low-carb twist on the classic treat. With a crispy exterior and a soft, cinnamon-infused interior, these bites are perfect for satisfying your sweet tooth without the guilt.

Equipment

Slow Cooker, Mixing Bowl, Whisk

Ingredients

- 200g Almond Flour
- 50g Coconut Flour
- 100g Erythritol
- 5g Baking Powder
- 2g Ground Cinnamon
- 3 Large Eggs
- 100ml Unsweetened Almond Milk
- 5ml Vanilla Extract
- 50g Butter, melted

Directions

1. In a mixing bowl, combine almond flour, coconut flour, erythritol, baking powder, and ground cinnamon.
2. In a separate bowl, whisk together eggs, almond milk, vanilla extract, and melted butter.
3. Gradually add the wet ingredients to the dry ingredients, stirring until a smooth batter forms.
4. Grease the slow cooker with a small amount of butter or cooking spray.
5. Pour the batter into the slow cooker, spreading it evenly.
6. Cover and cook on low for 2 hours, or until the churro bites are firm and golden.
7. Allow to cool slightly before cutting into bite-sized pieces.

Nutritional Information

Calories: 180, Protein: 6g, Carbohydrates: 5g, Fat: 15g, Fiber: 3g, Cholesterol: 55mg, Salt: 60mg, Potassium: 80mg

SLOW COOKER BUTTER PECAN ICE CREAM

Indulge in a creamy, low-carb delight with this slow cooker butter pecan ice cream. Rich and nutty, it's the perfect guilt-free dessert.

Equipment

Slow Cooker, Mixing Bowl, Whisk

Ingredients

- 500 ml Heavy Cream
- 250 ml Unsweetened Almond Milk
- 100 g Erythritol Sweetener
- 100 g Pecans, chopped
- 50 g Unsalted Butter
- 5 ml Vanilla Extract
- 2 g Salt

Directions

1. In a slow cooker, combine heavy cream, almond milk, erythritol, and salt. Whisk until well mixed.
2. Set the slow cooker to low heat and cook for 1.5 hours, stirring occasionally.
3. In a pan, melt butter over medium heat. Add pecans and toast until golden brown.
4. Stir in vanilla extract and toasted pecans into the slow cooker mixture.
5. Transfer the mixture to a freezer-safe container and freeze until firm.
6. Scoop and serve chilled.

Nutritional Information

Calories: 320, Protein: 3g, Carbohydrates: 5g, Fat: 33g, Fiber: 2g, Cholesterol: 70 mg, Salt: 150 mg, Potassium: 120 mg

SUGAR-FREE CHOCOLATE BROWNIES

Servings 8 | Prep: 15 min | Cook: 120 min

Indulge in these rich, fudgy brownies without the guilt. Perfectly crafted in a slow cooker, they are sugar-free and low in carbs, making them a delightful treat for any occasion.

Equipment

Slow Cooker, Mixing Bowl, Whisk

Ingredients

- 200 g Almond Flour
- 100 g Unsweetened Cocoa Powder
- 150 g Erythritol
- 100 g Unsalted Butter, melted
- 4 Large Eggs
- 1 tsp Vanilla Extract
- 1/2 tsp Baking Powder
- 1/4 tsp Salt
- 100 g Sugar-Free Dark Chocolate Chips

Directions

1. In a mixing bowl, whisk together almond flour, cocoa powder, erythritol, baking powder, and salt.
2. In another bowl, beat the eggs and mix in melted butter and vanilla extract.
3. Combine the wet and dry ingredients, stirring until smooth. Fold in the chocolate chips.
4. Line the slow cooker with parchment paper and pour the batter evenly into it.
5. Cover and cook on low for 2 hours or until a toothpick inserted in the center comes out clean.
6. Allow to cool before slicing into squares.

Nutritional Information

Calories: 250, Protein: 7g, Carbohydrates: 8g, Fat: 22g, Fiber: 4g, Cholesterol: 80 mg, Salt: 120 mg, Potassium: 150 mg

KETO COCONUT FLOUR MUG CAKE

Servings 1 | Prep: 5 min | Cook: 3 min

Indulge in a quick and satisfying low-carb dessert with this Keto Coconut Flour Mug Cake. Perfectly moist and rich, this treat is ideal for a guilt-free sweet craving.

Equipment

Microwave, Mug, Whisk

Ingredients

- 30 g Coconut Flour
- 15 g Unsweetened Cocoa Powder
- 5 g Baking Powder
- 1 Large Egg
- 30 ml Almond Milk
- 15 ml Coconut Oil, melted
- 10 ml Vanilla Extract
- 15 g Erythritol (or preferred low-carb sweetener)

Directions

1. In a mug, whisk together the coconut flour, cocoa powder, and baking powder.
2. Add the egg, almond milk, melted coconut oil, vanilla extract, and erythritol. Mix until smooth.
3. Microwave on high for 2-3 minutes, or until the cake has set and is cooked through.
4. Allow to cool slightly before enjoying.
5. Optionally, top with a dollop of whipped cream or a sprinkle of cocoa powder.

Nutritional Information

Calories: 220, Protein: 8g, Carbohydrates: 12g, Fat: 16g, Fiber: 8g, Cholesterol: 185 mg, Salt: 150 mg, Potassium: 180 mg

SLOW COOKER APPLE CINNAMON CRISP

Servings 6 | Prep: 15 min | Cook: 180 min

This delightful low-carb dessert combines the warmth of cinnamon with the natural sweetness of apples, all slow-cooked to perfection. It's a comforting treat that satisfies your sweet tooth without the carb overload.

Equipment

Slow Cooker, Mixing Bowl, Measuring Cups and Spoons

Ingredients

- 800 g apples, peeled, cored, and sliced
- 100 g almond flour
- 50 g chopped walnuts
- 50 g unsweetened shredded coconut
- 60 ml melted coconut oil
- 2 tsp ground cinnamon
- 1 tsp vanilla extract
- 1/4 tsp salt
- 30 g erythritol or preferred low-carb sweetener

Directions

1. In a mixing bowl, combine almond flour, walnuts, shredded coconut, melted coconut oil, cinnamon, vanilla extract, salt, and erythritol. Mix until crumbly.
2. Place the sliced apples in the slow cooker.
3. Evenly distribute the crumble mixture over the apples.
4. Cover and cook on low for 3 hours, or until apples are tender.
5. Serve warm, optionally with a dollop of whipped cream or low-carb ice cream.

Nutritional Information

Calories: 250, Protein: 4g, Carbohydrates: 18g, Fat: 20g, Fiber: 5g, Cholesterol: 0 mg, Salt: 100 mg, Potassium: 220 mg

SUGAR-FREE CHOCOLATE TRUFFLES

Servings 12 | Prep: 15 min | Cook: 60 min

Indulge in these rich, creamy, and decadent chocolate truffles without the guilt. Perfect for satisfying your sweet tooth while staying low carb.

Equipment

Slow Cooker, Mixing Bowl, Spoon

Ingredients

- 200 g Sugar-Free Dark Chocolate, chopped
- 100 ml Heavy Cream
- 50 g Unsalted Butter
- 1 tsp Vanilla Extract
- 30 g Unsweetened Cocoa Powder

Directions

1. Add the chopped chocolate, heavy cream, and butter to the slow cooker.
2. Set the slow cooker to low and let the mixture melt, stirring occasionally, for about 60 minutes.
3. Once melted, stir in the vanilla extract until well combined.
4. Transfer the mixture to a mixing bowl and refrigerate for 2 hours or until firm.
5. Scoop small amounts of the mixture and roll into balls.
6. Roll each truffle in unsweetened cocoa powder to coat.

Nutritional Information

Calories: 120, Protein: 2g, Carbohydrates: 4g, Fat: 11g, Fiber: 2g, Cholesterol: 15 mg, Salt: 10 mg, Potassium: 100 mg

SLOW COOKER ALMOND JOY BARS

Servings 8 | Prep: 15 min | Cook: 120 min

Indulge in these rich and satisfying Almond Joy Bars, a low-carb delight that combines the classic flavors of coconut, almonds, and chocolate, all effortlessly prepared in your slow cooker.

Equipment

Slow Cooker, Mixing Bowl, Parchment Paper

Ingredients

- 200 g Unsweetened Shredded Coconut
- 100 g Almonds, chopped
- 150 g Sugar-Free Dark Chocolate Chips
- 100 ml Coconut Milk
- 50 g Almond Butter
- 30 g Erythritol
- 5 ml Vanilla Extract

Directions

1. Line the slow cooker with parchment paper for easy removal.
2. In a mixing bowl, combine shredded coconut, chopped almonds, and erythritol.
3. Melt the almond butter and chocolate chips together in a microwave or double boiler, then stir in the coconut milk and vanilla extract until smooth.
4. Pour the chocolate mixture over the coconut mixture and stir until well combined.
5. Spread the mixture evenly in the slow cooker.
6. Cover and cook on low for 2 hours, or until set.
7. Allow to cool completely before cutting into bars.

Nutritional Information

Calories: 250, Protein: 5g, Carbohydrates: 8g, Fat: 22g, Fiber: 4g, Cholesterol: 0 mg, Salt: 10 mg, Potassium: 150 mg

KETO TIRAMISU

Servings 8 | Prep: 20 min | Cook: 180 min

Indulge in a classic Italian dessert with a keto twist, offering rich layers of creamy mascarpone and coffee-soaked almond flour cake, all crafted effortlessly in your slow cooker.

Equipment

Slow Cooker, Mixing Bowls, Whisk

Ingredients

- 200 g Almond Flour
- 100 g Erythritol
- 5 Eggs
- 250 g Mascarpone Cheese
- 200 ml Strong Brewed Coffee
- 50 ml Heavy Cream
- 10 g Cocoa Powder
- 5 ml Vanilla Extract
- 2 g Baking Powder
- Pinch of Salt

Directions

1. In a mixing bowl, whisk together almond flour, erythritol, baking powder, and salt.
2. Separate eggs; beat yolks with vanilla extract and fold into dry ingredients. Whisk whites until stiff peaks form and gently fold into the mixture.
3. Pour batter into a greased slow cooker and cook on low for 2 hours or until set.
4. Once cooled, slice the cake horizontally. Soak each layer with brewed coffee.
5. In another bowl, mix mascarpone, heavy cream, and a bit of erythritol until smooth. Layer mascarpone mixture between cake layers.
6. Dust the top with cocoa powder and refrigerate for at least 1 hour before serving.

Nutritional Information

Calories: 320, Protein: 9g, Carbohydrates: 6g, Fat: 28g, Fiber: 3g, Cholesterol: 140 mg, Salt: 120 mg, Potassium: 150 mg

DRINKS

SLOW COOKER KETO HOT CHOCOLATE

Servings 4 | Prep: 10 min | Cook: 120 min

Indulge in a rich and creamy keto hot chocolate, perfect for cozy evenings. This low-carb delight is effortlessly made in your slow cooker, ensuring a smooth and velvety texture with every sip.

Equipment

Slow Cooker, Whisk, Ladle

Ingredients

- 800 ml unsweetened almond milk
- 100 g dark chocolate (85% cocoa or higher), chopped
- 60 ml heavy cream
- 30 g unsweetened cocoa powder
- 2 g vanilla extract
- 2 g stevia or preferred low-carb sweetener
- Pinch of salt

Directions

1. Add almond milk, chopped dark chocolate, heavy cream, and cocoa powder to the slow cooker.
2. Whisk the mixture until the cocoa powder is fully dissolved.
3. Set the slow cooker to low and cook for 2 hours, stirring occasionally.
4. After 2 hours, add vanilla extract, stevia, and a pinch of salt. Stir well.
5. Ladle the hot chocolate into mugs and serve warm.

Nutritional Information

Calories: 210, Protein: 5g, Carbohydrates: 8g, Fat: 18g, Fiber: 4g, Cholesterol: 20 mg, Salt: 150 mg, Potassium: 250 mg

LOW CARB PUMPKIN SPICE LATTE

Servings 4 | Prep: 10 min | Cook: 120 min

A cozy, autumn-inspired drink that combines the rich flavors of pumpkin and spices, perfect for a low-carb lifestyle.

Equipment

Slow Cooker, Whisk, Ladle

Ingredients

- 500 ml Unsweetened Almond Milk
- 100 ml Brewed Espresso or Strong Coffee
- 100 g Pumpkin Puree
- 2 g Ground Cinnamon
- 1 g Ground Nutmeg
- 1 g Ground Ginger
- 1 g Ground Cloves
- 5 ml Vanilla Extract
- 30 g Erythritol or Preferred Low-Carb Sweetener
- 60 ml Heavy Cream (optional, for topping)

Directions

1. In the slow cooker, combine almond milk, espresso, pumpkin puree, cinnamon, nutmeg, ginger, cloves, vanilla extract, and erythritol.
2. Whisk the mixture until all ingredients are well combined.
3. Set the slow cooker to low and cook for 2 hours, stirring occasionally.
4. Once done, ladle the latte into mugs.
5. Optionally, top with whipped heavy cream and a sprinkle of cinnamon before serving.

Nutritional Information

Calories: 50, Protein: 1g, Carbohydrates: 3g, Fat: 4g, Fiber: 1g, Cholesterol: 10 mg, Salt: 50 mg, Potassium: 100 mg

SLOW COOKER SUGAR-FREE APPLE CIDER

Servings 6 | Prep: 10 min | Cook: 240 min

Warm up with this comforting, sugar-free apple cider, perfect for cozy gatherings or a quiet evening at home. The slow cooker infuses the flavors beautifully, making it a delightful low-carb treat.

Equipment

Slow Cooker, Strainer, Ladle

Ingredients

- 1.5 kg Apples, quartered
- 2 l Water
- 2 Cinnamon Sticks
- 5 g Whole Cloves
- 1 Orange, sliced
- 5 ml Vanilla Extract
- 30 g Erythritol (optional, for sweetness)

Directions

1. Place the quartered apples, cinnamon sticks, cloves, and orange slices into the slow cooker.
2. Pour in the water, ensuring all ingredients are submerged.
3. Cover and cook on low for 4 hours, allowing the flavors to meld.
4. After cooking, use a strainer to remove the solids, pressing gently to extract all the liquid.
5. Stir in the vanilla extract and erythritol, if using, until well combined.
6. Serve warm, garnished with a cinnamon stick or orange slice if desired.

Nutritional Information

Calories: 50, Protein: 0.5g, Carbohydrates: 12g, Fat: 0g, Fiber: 3g, Cholesterol: 0 mg, Salt: 5 mg, Potassium: 150 mg

KETO VANILLA CHAI TEA

Servings 4 | Prep: 10 min | Cook: 120 min

This comforting Keto Vanilla Chai Tea combines aromatic spices with creamy vanilla for a soothing, low-carb beverage perfect for any time of day.

Equipment

Slow Cooker, Whisk, Strainer

Ingredients

- 1 l Water
- 4 Chai Tea Bags
- 200 ml Unsweetened Almond Milk
- 1 Vanilla Bean, split and scraped
- 2 g Ground Cinnamon
- 2 g Ground Ginger
- 1 g Ground Cloves
- 2 g Stevia or preferred low-carb sweetener
- 1 g Ground Black Pepper

Directions

1. Add water, chai tea bags, vanilla bean, cinnamon, ginger, cloves, and black pepper to the slow cooker.
2. Cover and cook on low for 2 hours.
3. Remove tea bags and vanilla bean.
4. Stir in almond milk and sweetener, whisking until well combined.
5. Strain the tea into cups and serve warm.

Nutritional Information

Calories: 25, Protein: 1g, Carbohydrates: 2g, Fat: 1g, Fiber: 1g, Cholesterol: 0 mg, Salt: 50 mg, Potassium: 50 mg

SLOW COOKER BULLETPROOF COFFEE

Servings 4 | Prep: 5 min | Cook: 60 min

This rich and creamy bulletproof coffee is perfect for a low-carb lifestyle. Made effortlessly in a slow cooker, it combines the boldness of coffee with the richness of butter and coconut oil for a satisfying start to your day.

Equipment

Slow Cooker, Blender, Measuring Cups

Ingredients

- 1 liter brewed coffee
- 50 g unsalted butter
- 50 g coconut oil
- 5 ml vanilla extract
- 2 g ground cinnamon

Directions

1. Brew 1 liter of your favorite coffee.
2. Pour the brewed coffee into the slow cooker.
3. Add the unsalted butter, coconut oil, vanilla extract, and ground cinnamon to the slow cooker.
4. Cover and set the slow cooker to low. Let it cook for 60 minutes, stirring occasionally.
5. Once done, carefully transfer the mixture to a blender. Blend on high for 30 seconds until frothy.
6. Pour into mugs and enjoy your creamy, low-carb bulletproof coffee.

Nutritional Information

Calories: 210, Protein: 0.5g, Carbohydrates: 1g, Fat: 23g, Fiber: 0g, Cholesterol: 30mg, Salt: 5mg, Potassium: 120mg

SUGAR-FREE LEMON GINGER TEA

Servings 4 | Prep: 10 min | Cook: 120 min

This refreshing and invigorating tea combines the zesty flavor of lemon with the warming spice of ginger, all without any added sugar. Perfect for a soothing drink any time of day.

Equipment

Slow Cooker, Knife, Cutting Board, Strainer

Ingredients

- 1 liter water
- 50 g fresh ginger, sliced
- 1 lemon, sliced
- 2 cinnamon sticks
- 5 g stevia or preferred sugar substitute
- 5 g loose leaf green tea or 2 tea bags

Directions

1. Add water, ginger slices, lemon slices, and cinnamon sticks to the slow cooker.
2. Set the slow cooker to low and let it simmer for 2 hours.
3. After 2 hours, add the stevia and green tea. Let it steep for an additional 10 minutes.
4. Strain the tea into cups, discarding the solids.
5. Serve hot or let it cool and serve over ice for a refreshing iced tea.

Nutritional Information

Calories: 5, Protein: 0g, Carbohydrates: 1g, Fat: 0g, Fiber: 0g, Cholesterol: 0mg, Salt: 0mg, Potassium: 10mg

KETO STRAWBERRY MILKSHAKE

Servings 4 | Prep: 10 min | Cook: 0 min

Indulge in a creamy, low-carb strawberry milkshake that satisfies your sweet cravings while keeping you on track with your keto lifestyle. This refreshing drink is perfect for a quick breakfast or a delightful afternoon treat.

Equipment

Blender, Measuring Cups, Measuring Spoons

Ingredients

- 200 g Fresh Strawberries, hulled
- 500 ml Unsweetened Almond Milk
- 100 ml Heavy Cream
- 30 g Erythritol (or preferred low-carb sweetener)
- 5 ml Vanilla Extract
- 200 g Ice Cubes

Directions

1. Add the fresh strawberries, almond milk, heavy cream, erythritol, and vanilla extract into the blender.
2. Blend on high speed until the mixture is smooth and creamy.
3. Add the ice cubes to the blender and blend again until the ice is crushed and the milkshake reaches your desired consistency.
4. Taste and adjust sweetness if necessary by adding more erythritol.
5. Pour into glasses and serve immediately for a refreshing keto-friendly treat.

Nutritional Information

Calories: 120, Protein: 2g, Carbohydrates: 5g, Fat: 10g, Fiber: 2g, Cholesterol: 25 mg, Salt: 50 mg, Potassium: 150 mg

SLOW COOKER TURMERIC GOLDEN MILK

Servings 4 | Prep: 5 min | Cook: 120 min

Warm and soothing, this golden milk combines the anti-inflammatory benefits of turmeric with the creamy richness of coconut milk, perfect for a cozy evening.

Equipment

Slow Cooker, Whisk, Measuring Cups

Ingredients

- 800 ml Coconut Milk
- 500 ml Water
- 10 g Fresh Turmeric, grated
- 5 g Fresh Ginger, grated
- 5 g Ground Cinnamon
- 2 g Ground Black Pepper
- 15 ml Honey (optional)
- 5 ml Vanilla Extract

Directions

1. Combine coconut milk and water in the slow cooker.
2. Add grated turmeric, ginger, cinnamon, and black pepper. Whisk until well mixed.
3. Cover and cook on low for 2 hours, stirring occasionally.
4. Stir in honey and vanilla extract before serving.
5. Strain the mixture into mugs and enjoy warm.

Nutritional Information

Calories: 180, Protein: 2g, Carbohydrates: 6g, Fat: 16g, Fiber: 1g, Cholesterol: 0 mg, Salt: 20 mg, Potassium: 150 mg

LOW CARB BERRY SMOOTHIE

This refreshing low carb berry smoothie is a perfect blend of tangy berries and creamy coconut milk, offering a delightful and nutritious start to your day.

Equipment

Blender, Measuring Cups, Measuring Spoons

Ingredients

- 200 g Mixed Berries (fresh or frozen)
- 400 ml Coconut Milk
- 100 ml Water
- 30 g Chia Seeds
- 10 g Stevia or preferred low-carb sweetener
- 5 ml Vanilla Extract

Directions

1. Add the mixed berries, coconut milk, and water to the blender.
2. Sprinkle in the chia seeds and add the stevia.
3. Pour in the vanilla extract for added flavor.
4. Blend on high speed until smooth and creamy.
5. Taste and adjust sweetness if necessary.
6. Pour into glasses and serve immediately.

Nutritional Information

Calories: 120, Protein: 2g, Carbohydrates: 8g, Fat: 10g, Fiber: 4g, Cholesterol: 0 mg, Salt: 10 mg, Potassium: 150 mg

KETO ICED MATCHA LATTE

A refreshing and creamy iced matcha latte that's perfect for a low-carb lifestyle. This drink combines the earthy flavors of matcha with the richness of coconut milk, all prepared effortlessly in a slow cooker.

Equipment

Slow Cooker, Whisk, Measuring Cups

Ingredients

- 500 ml Coconut Milk
- 10 g Matcha Powder
- 30 ml Hot Water
- 10 g Erythritol (or preferred low-carb sweetener)
- 5 ml Vanilla Extract
- Ice Cubes (as needed)

Directions

1. In a small bowl, whisk the matcha powder with hot water until smooth and no lumps remain.
2. Pour the coconut milk into the slow cooker and set it to low heat.
3. Add the matcha mixture, erythritol, and vanilla extract to the slow cooker, stirring well to combine.
4. Allow the mixture to heat for about 10 minutes, stirring occasionally until the erythritol is fully dissolved.
5. Remove from heat and let it cool slightly. Fill two glasses with ice cubes and pour the matcha latte over the ice.
6. Stir well before serving and enjoy your refreshing keto iced matcha latte.

Nutritional Information

Calories: 150, Protein: 2g, Carbohydrates: 3g, Fat: 14g, Fiber: 1g, Cholesterol: 0mg, Salt: 15mg, Potassium: 250mg

SLOW COOKER SPICED ALMOND MILK

Servings 4 | Prep: 10 min | Cook: 240 min

Warm and comforting, this spiced almond milk is perfect for cozy evenings. Infused with aromatic spices, it's a delightful low-carb treat.

Equipment

Slow Cooker, Whisk, Strainer

Ingredients

- 1 liter Almond Milk
- 5 g Ground Cinnamon
- 2 g Ground Nutmeg
- 5 g Vanilla Extract
- 30 g Erythritol (or preferred low-carb sweetener)
- 2 g Ground Cloves

Directions

1. Pour the almond milk into the slow cooker.
2. Add ground cinnamon, nutmeg, vanilla extract, erythritol, and ground cloves.
3. Whisk the ingredients together until well combined.
4. Cover and cook on low for 4 hours, stirring occasionally.
5. Strain the mixture to remove any spice sediments before serving.

Nutritional Information

Calories: 45, Protein: 1g, Carbohydrates: 2g, Fat: 3g, Fiber: 1g, Cholesterol: 0 mg, Salt: 150 mg, Potassium: 180 mg

LOW CARB ELECTROLYTE LEMONADE

Servings 4 | Prep: 10 min | Cook: 120 min

This refreshing and hydrating lemonade is perfect for replenishing electrolytes while keeping your carb intake low. The slow cooker infuses the flavors beautifully, making it a delightful drink for any occasion.

Equipment

Slow Cooker, Measuring Cups, Strainer

Ingredients

- 1 l Water
- 100 ml Fresh Lemon Juice
- 30 g Erythritol (or preferred low-carb sweetener)
- 2 g Sea Salt
- 2 g Magnesium Powder (optional)
- 5 g Fresh Mint Leaves

Directions

1. Pour the water into the slow cooker.
2. Add fresh lemon juice, erythritol, sea salt, and magnesium powder. Stir until the erythritol is dissolved.
3. Add fresh mint leaves to the mixture.
4. Cover and set the slow cooker to low. Let it infuse for 2 hours.
5. Strain the lemonade to remove mint leaves and any pulp.
6. Chill in the refrigerator before serving or serve over ice.

Nutritional Information

Calories: 5, Protein: 0g, Carbohydrates: 1g, Fat: 0g, Fiber: 0g, Cholesterol: 0 mg, Salt: 500 mg, Potassium: 20 mg

KETO BUTTERED RUM COFFEE

Servings 4 | Prep: 10 min | Cook: 120 min

A rich and creamy low-carb coffee delight with a hint of rum and butter, perfect for cozy mornings or an indulgent afternoon treat.

Equipment

Slow Cooker, Whisk, Measuring Cups

Ingredients

- 500 ml brewed coffee
- 60 ml dark rum
- 50 g unsalted butter
- 60 ml heavy cream
- 1 tsp vanilla extract
- 1 tsp ground cinnamon
- 2 tbsp erythritol or preferred low-carb sweetener

Directions

1. Pour the brewed coffee into the slow cooker.
2. Add dark rum, unsalted butter, heavy cream, vanilla extract, and ground cinnamon.
3. Stir in erythritol until fully dissolved.
4. Cover and cook on low for 2 hours, allowing flavors to meld.
5. Whisk the mixture before serving to ensure even distribution of ingredients.
6. Pour into mugs and enjoy warm.

Nutritional Information

Calories: 150, Protein: 1g, Carbohydrates: 2g, Fat: 14g, Fiber: 0g, Cholesterol: 35 mg, Salt: 20 mg, Potassium: 100 mg

SLOW COOKER RASPBERRY HIBISCUS TEA

Servings 6 | Prep: 10 min | Cook: 120 min

This refreshing and aromatic Raspberry Hibiscus Tea is a delightful low-carb beverage, perfect for any time of the day. The slow cooker infuses the flavors beautifully, creating a vibrant and soothing drink.

Equipment

Slow Cooker, Strainer, Pitcher

Ingredients

- 1 liter water
- 50 g dried hibiscus flowers
- 100 g fresh raspberries
- 30 g erythritol (or preferred low-carb sweetener)
- 1 cinnamon stick
- 5 ml vanilla extract

Directions

1. Pour the water into the slow cooker and set it to low heat.
2. Add the dried hibiscus flowers, fresh raspberries, erythritol, and cinnamon stick to the slow cooker.
3. Cover and let it simmer for 2 hours, allowing the flavors to meld.
4. After cooking, strain the mixture into a pitcher to remove solids.
5. Stir in the vanilla extract and let the tea cool before serving over ice or warm.

Nutritional Information

Calories: 10, Protein: 0g, Carbohydrates: 2g, Fat: 0g, Fiber: 1g, Cholesterol: 0mg, Salt: 0mg, Potassium: 20mg

SUGAR-FREE EGGNOG

Indulge in the creamy richness of traditional eggnog without the sugar. This slow-cooked version is perfect for holiday gatherings or a cozy night in.

Equipment

Slow Cooker, Whisk, Measuring Cups

Ingredients

- 500 ml Unsweetened Almond Milk
- 250 ml Heavy Cream
- 4 Large Eggs
- 50 g Erythritol
- 1 tsp Vanilla Extract
- 1/2 tsp Ground Nutmeg
- 1/4 tsp Ground Cinnamon
- 1/4 tsp Salt

Directions

1. In a slow cooker, combine almond milk and heavy cream.
2. In a separate bowl, whisk together eggs, erythritol, vanilla extract, nutmeg, cinnamon, and salt until smooth.
3. Gradually add the egg mixture to the slow cooker, whisking continuously to combine.
4. Set the slow cooker to low and cook for 2 hours, stirring occasionally.
5. Once thickened, transfer the eggnog to a pitcher and refrigerate until chilled.
6. Serve cold, garnished with a sprinkle of nutmeg if desired.

Nutritional Information

Calories: 180, Protein: 5g, Carbohydrates: 3g, Fat: 17g, Fiber: 0g, Cholesterol: 150 mg, Salt: 150 mg, Potassium: 100 mg

KETO MOCHA FRAPPE

Indulge in a creamy, chocolatey coffee delight that's low in carbs and perfect for a refreshing treat. This Keto Mocha Frappe combines rich flavors with a smooth texture, all prepared effortlessly in your slow cooker.

Equipment

Slow Cooker, Blender, Measuring Cups

Ingredients

- 500 ml brewed coffee, cooled
- 200 ml unsweetened almond milk
- 50 g unsweetened cocoa powder
- 60 ml heavy cream
- 30 g erythritol or preferred low-carb sweetener
- 1 tsp vanilla extract
- 100 g ice cubes

Directions

1. In the slow cooker, combine brewed coffee, almond milk, cocoa powder, heavy cream, erythritol, and vanilla extract.
2. Stir the mixture well until the cocoa powder and sweetener are fully dissolved.
3. Cover and set the slow cooker to the "Keep Warm" setting for 10 minutes to blend flavors.
4. Transfer the mixture to a blender, add ice cubes, and blend until smooth and frothy.
5. Pour into glasses and serve immediately.

Nutritional Information

Calories: 85, Protein: 2g, Carbohydrates: 4g, Fat: 8g, Fiber: 2g, Cholesterol: 20 mg, Salt: 50 mg, Potassium: 150 mg

SLOW COOKER CINNAMON VANILLA ALMOND MILK

Servings 4 | Prep: 10 min | Cook: 240 min

Indulge in the creamy and aromatic delight of homemade almond milk, infused with the warm flavors of cinnamon and vanilla. Perfect for a cozy evening or as a refreshing morning drink.

Equipment

Slow Cooker, Blender, Fine Mesh Strainer or Nut Milk Bag

Ingredients

- 200 g raw almonds
- 1 l water
- 5 ml vanilla extract
- 5 g ground cinnamon
- 2 g salt
- 10 g erythritol (optional, for sweetness)

Directions

1. Rinse the almonds thoroughly and place them in the slow cooker.
2. Add water, vanilla extract, ground cinnamon, and salt to the slow cooker.
3. Cover and cook on low for 4 hours, allowing the flavors to meld.
4. Once cooked, let the mixture cool slightly, then transfer to a blender.
5. Blend on high until smooth and creamy.
6. Strain the mixture through a fine mesh strainer or nut milk bag to remove solids.
7. Sweeten with erythritol if desired, and serve chilled or warm.

Nutritional Information

Calories: 120, Protein: 4g, Carbohydrates: 5g, Fat: 10g, Fiber: 2g, Cholesterol: 0 mg, Salt: 150 mg, Potassium: 200 mg

SUGAR-FREE GINGERBREAD LATTE

Servings 4 | Prep: 10 min | Cook: 120 min

Warm and comforting, this sugar-free gingerbread latte combines the rich flavors of ginger, cinnamon, and nutmeg, perfect for a cozy day.

Equipment

Slow Cooker, Whisk, Measuring Cups and Spoons

Ingredients

- 500 ml Unsweetened Almond Milk
- 250 ml Brewed Coffee
- 60 ml Heavy Cream
- 2 g Ground Ginger
- 2 g Ground Cinnamon
- 1 g Ground Nutmeg
- 5 ml Vanilla Extract
- 10 ml Sugar-Free Sweetener (liquid form)
- 2 g Ground Cloves (optional)

Directions

1. Pour the almond milk, brewed coffee, and heavy cream into the slow cooker.
2. Whisk in the ground ginger, cinnamon, nutmeg, and cloves until well combined.
3. Add the vanilla extract and sugar-free sweetener, stirring gently.
4. Cover and cook on low for 2 hours, allowing the flavors to meld.
5. Stir the mixture before serving, ensuring even distribution of spices.
6. Pour into mugs and enjoy warm.

Nutritional Information

Calories: 85, Protein: 2g, Carbohydrates: 3g, Fat: 7g, Fiber: 1g, Cholesterol: 20 mg, Salt: 60 mg, Potassium: 120 mg

KETO STRAWBERRY LEMONADE

Servings 4 | Prep: 10 min | Cook: 60 min

This refreshing Keto Strawberry Lemonade is a perfect blend of tangy lemons and sweet strawberries, all slow-cooked to perfection. A delightful low-carb drink to quench your thirst.

Equipment

Slow Cooker, Blender, Fine Mesh Strainer

Ingredients

- 500 g fresh strawberries, hulled and halved
- 250 ml fresh lemon juice (about 4-5 lemons)
- 750 ml water
- 60 g erythritol (or preferred low-carb sweetener)
- 1 lemon, sliced for garnish
- Ice cubes, as needed

Directions

1. Place the strawberries, lemon juice, water, and erythritol in the slow cooker.
2. Stir the mixture to combine all ingredients well.
3. Cover and cook on low for 60 minutes until strawberries are soft.
4. Use a blender to puree the mixture until smooth.
5. Strain the lemonade through a fine mesh strainer to remove pulp and seeds.
6. Chill in the refrigerator or serve immediately over ice.
7. Garnish with lemon slices before serving.

Nutritional Information

Calories: 35, Protein: 0.5g, Carbohydrates: 8g, Fat: 0g, Fiber: 2g, Cholesterol: 0 mg, Salt: 5 mg, Potassium: 150 mg

SLOW COOKER HERBAL DETOX TEA

Servings 4 | Prep: 10 min | Cook: 240 min

This soothing herbal detox tea is perfect for cleansing and rejuvenating your body. The slow cooker method allows the flavors to meld beautifully, creating a comforting and aromatic beverage.

Equipment

Slow Cooker, Strainer, Measuring Cups

Ingredients

- 1 l Water
- 10 g Fresh Ginger, sliced
- 5 g Fresh Turmeric, sliced
- 5 g Dried Chamomile Flowers
- 5 g Dried Peppermint Leaves
- 5 g Dried Hibiscus Flowers
- 1 Cinnamon Stick
- 1 Lemon, sliced
- 10 ml Honey (optional)

Directions

1. Add water to the slow cooker.
2. Add ginger, turmeric, chamomile, peppermint, hibiscus, and cinnamon stick to the water.
3. Stir gently to combine all ingredients.
4. Cover and cook on low for 4 hours.
5. Strain the tea into a teapot or pitcher, discarding solids.
6. Add lemon slices and honey if desired, stirring to combine.
7. Serve warm or chilled, as preferred.

Nutritional Information

Calories: 15, Protein: 0g, Carbohydrates: 4g, Fat: 0g, Fiber: 0g, Cholesterol: 0 mg, Salt: 5 mg, Potassium: 50 mg

Printed in Dunstable, United Kingdom